THE LTA GUIDE TO
BETTER TENNIS

Published in the same series by Pan Books

The PGA European Tour Guide to Better Golf

Forthcoming

The SRA and WSRA Guide to Better Squash
The British Ski Federation Guide to Better Skiing

THE LTA
GUIDE TO BETTER
TENNIS

CHARLES APPLEWHAITE

JANE POYNDER

Photographs by Tommy Hindley

Pan Books   London and Sydney

Contents

PART TWO   **THE USE OF SPIN**

Jane Poynder
and
Charles Applewhaite

PART THREE   STROKE VARIATIONS

PART FOUR   **MATCHPLAY STRATEGY**

VIRGINIA WADE

Foreword

Virginia Wade won the Wimbledon Ladies Singles Championship in 1977

Tennis has developed by leaps and bounds since I first started to play. Its complexion has changed from a rather select amateur sport to a vibrantly competitive one. However the essential qualities have remained – the sheer pleasure of playing the game and the desire to win.

It is a truly thrilling time to take up the game. There is endless motivation really to excel, plus the fact that there is a pool of knowledge available at hand to help one.

To me the most important factor to set one on the right track is good basic technique. The game has been highly analysed and there are many more coaches able to deliver that expertise. In addition, with all the television coverage of top world class tennis, there is no shortage of good examples to imitate. Good technique improves the quality of the game throughout all levels of playing.

Now if you have the talent, good technique and desire to go to the top, all that's necessary is practice, practice, practice plus real determination. The sport presents so many challenges with enormous satisfaction and rewards for those who have the courage to go after them.

This book is an excellent manual of the latest theories and technical information available. From here the whole world can open up.

9

Introduction

As Britain's National Team Manager I am often being asked the question: what makes a Wimbledon champion? What are the main attributes of the great players of today? While there are many answers and opinions, I believe there are some fundamental common traits in the great champions.

Firstly, the main ingredient must be desire. A desire to win – to learn – to practise – to train – to come back after defeat – to fight – to have true match winning instincts and, finally, the desire to prove you are the best.

Secondly, a love for the actual game. Particularly at a young age there are so many other distractions, sports and activities and so often losing too often means that a player loses interest. But the great players have an insatiable appetite for the game.

Another ingredient is athleticism. Movement, agility, balance, stamina, speed and strength are all traits of champions in many sports, but they are essential in tennis, which is physically such a demanding game.

Tennis is also mentally very demanding, so attitude and temperament are vital ingredients of champions, as is the ability to have the right technique in order to

Paul Hutchins is Britain's Davis Cup Captain and National Team Manager

execute the right shot at the right time.

All these qualities that a champion must have can be wrapped up and called talent, and it is the ability to bring them together at the same time which makes the champions so inspiring to players from beginners upwards.

As I write this introduction it seems that not only the tennis orientated public throughout the world, but people of all ages and all walks of life are avidly following the fortunes of a young man called Boris Becker. In a recent article on the front page of the *International Herald Tribune* is a picture of the young man himself with a large banner headline 'German Youth . . . A return to Conservatism'. The article explains how, even at only 18 years of age, Boris Becker is having a major influence on German society and is a 'symbol of identification for the post peace movement generation'.

This is heavy stuff, but we have always needed leaders to follow, people to admire; and we are privileged at this time to have someone like Becker to look up to. Tennis, as a sport, can only gain by such admiration and adulation.

Even the younger generation, reading this book, will probably remember another player who was a modern superstar of sport, Bjorn Borg. Sweden as a country has gained so much from Borg and has produced a new generation of world class players that is unrivalled. It is interesting to look at some statistics. From Sweden's population of 8.5 million, where 2.5 million play a variety of sports, there are 54,000 juniors playing tennis out of a total of 400,000 players. There are 1400 indoor courts and 2,800 outdoor courts, and the key is that virtually every club in Sweden is totally junior orientated, with 60 full time teaching professional and 8,000 amateur coaches, all participating in a structural junior development programme throughout the country. This system, as well as the interest in Bjorn Borg, whose success literally doubled the number of players in the game in Sweden between 1973 and 1980, has left every other country standing and scratching their heads in an effor to emulate the Swedish system.

Every country in the world is trying to produce a Becker or a Borg, as players like these can spearhead national interest in the game; but most countries admit that, whatever training, coaching and development system they have, the production of a Wimbledon champion is a unique occurrence, has no set guide lines and that whatever system there is, players like Borg, Navratilova and Becker will emerge.

This book, *The LTA Guide to Better Tennis*, is not *about* the Beckers or Navratilovas, but uses photos of the great players to illustrate how they achieve their success. The book is an excellent tool for beginners and also experienced players who want to improve and to learn more about the game. It covers many aspects of tennis, from the very basic techniques to the tactics used in singles and in doubles. It explains some of the most common faults and how to correct them, and offers advice on fitness, mental preparation and, very importantly, how to practise.

When you think of it, we all spend much more time on the practice court than playing matches, so this is an important area if you are keen to improve. Why not be more specific and learn some of the drills that

In 1985, at the age of seventeen, West Germany's Boris Becker became the youngest ever winner of the Wimbledon Singles Championship

can make practising more interesting? Select the right partner, and plan your practice sessions so that you can concentrate on strengthening your weaknesses and broadening your range of shots.

Even the top players have to put in hours and hours of practice, just concentrating on doing the basics very well. They all have different ways of hitting the ball, but the basic requirements of a good comfortable grip – watching the ball – early racket preparation on the ground strokes – punching the ball in front on the volley and throwing the racket head at the ball on service are essential, whatever style they use. Eventually, when you become a reasonably good player you can move on to refining these basics using top spin and

slice and adopting different matchplay strategies. The book will help in all these areas.

The Lawn Tennis Association is, I know, pleased to be associated with this book. When I started working for the LTA there were very few members of staff and, personally, as National Team Manager and Davis Cup Captain I found myself to be 'chief cook and bottle washer', looking after all aspects of the British National Teams and players, both male and female, from 12 upwards. Gradually, and particularly over the last 5 years, we have become much more organised and professionally run and, for example, we now have a Director of Coaching – Charles Applewhaite, who wrote this book with Jane Poynder. We now also have a proper structure of tennis coaching and development in Britain, at county, regional and national level. It is not yet perfect by any means and we can still learn from other countries who have particularly good club systems with plenty of indoor facilities, and clubs who are more junior orientated than Britain is at present. But I am optimistic that tennis will become increasingly popular here and that we will eventually satisfy the general public's desire for a new Wimbledon champion. Who knows, perhaps somewhere there's a young player reading this book who will become a future Wimbledon champion, and will look back and say, 'it was *The LTA Guide to Better Tennis* that started me off', I'd like to think it could happen.

Paul Hutchins
January 1986

CHARLES APPLEWHAITE

Getting started

Whether you are about to start playing this marvellous game or are already an experienced player, it is important that you look carefully at your choice of tennis equipment. This chapter is designed to give you some help in making decisions about rackets, clothing, balls etc.

Rackets

Choosing a racket even for an established player is at any time an important decision but the beginner may be totally bewildered by the variety of rackets available. There are wood, metal, fibre glass, aluminium, graphite etc; and if that is not enough, there are composite rackets made from a mixture of materials. The advantages and disadvantages of the different materials are hard to define but generally it is fair to say that wood – the traditional material – has very sound properties and the new materials have been used to try to improve upon it.

The graphite or composite racket tends to give the player more power but results in a slight loss of control. As a rough guide a player who hits the ball hard but lacks control should buy a wood racket. Conversely a player who is safe and controlled but lacks power should be looking for a graphite or composite racket.

There are three basic sizes of racket head – normal, mid-size and jumbo. Mid-size and jumbo were developed to try to improve upon the standard size of racket head by giving the player a bigger hitting area. In general, the larger racket head helps volleying, gives a little more power and a larger 'sweet spot' or hitting area, all of which increase a player's confidence. However, it does tend to be a little more cumbersome to use on service and smash.

The racket stringing is generally either nylon, synthetic, or gut. Gut (which is made from sheep's intestines) has fine playing qualities. Unfortunately it is quite expensive and it is fragile, especially in

When John McEnroe first appeared at Wimbledon in 1977 he was playing with a wooden racket.

for small children and finally special plastic rackets for Short Tennis for very young children. The weight of full-size rackets generally varies between 13–15oz (325–375g) and the grip size from 4¼" – 4¾" (105–120mm). Most types of racket come in a range of different weights with various grip sizes available, so you need to think hard about the size and weight that feels best for you.

As a general guide the beginner should purchase a racket that is not too expensive, then it won't be too disastrous if you have made a mistake (although it is false economy to purchase the cheapest available). The material used is at this stage not too important. The important thing is that the racket should not be too heavy, nor the grip too large. To find the right grip for you, make sure that your thumb and second finger overlap on the racket by approximately 1" – 1½" (25–40mm). Always ensure that you have a firm easy grip on the racket and can swing it without any discomfort.

It is most unwise to buy a racket for a youngster to 'grow into' because it is highly likely that by the time he has 'grown into' the racket he will have given up the sport because of lack of success. The established player will decide gradually what kind of racket suits him best, but bear in mind that if you do change your racket material, head size, weight, grip, etc. it will take a little time for a new racket to begin to feel comfortable. It is unwise to economise too much on the choice of racket as it will have a major effect on your enjoyment of the game.

damp conditions or on gritty courts. Nylon or synthetic string is a man-made alternative to gut and is highly durable and relatively inexpensive. There are many different variations on the synthetic strings and the better ones do have many of the qualities of natural gut.

Buying a racket is like buying clothes. You obviously need to have a good fit to feel comfortable. Tennis rackets are generally made in four main sizes. Full size for adults, junior for youngsters, small junior

Balls

You now have the racket and you need something to hit. How do you know which tennis ball is suitable for you? There are two main types of tennis ball: normal balls and pressureless balls. Normal tennis balls have air sealed inside them, but over a period of time the air gradually escapes and they become softer. Pressureless tennis balls have a harder outside casing and a vacuum inside. They do not go soft but they feel heavier on the strings and are more difficult to control. To complicate matters the normal tennis balls are divided into two groups, boxed or loose tennis balls, and those in pressurised cans. Tennis balls sealed in pressurised cans have an indefinite shelf life in the shop and will not start to deteriorate until the can is opened and the pressure released. These balls are obviously more suitable for storing for periods of time as long as the seal is not broken.

Clothing

You now have the racket and the balls but what should you wear? Tennis clothing is now available in a tremendous variety of styles and colours. To be on the safe side it is better to purchase clothing that is mainly white as many clubs still do not accept coloured clothing on the court. You will need a tennis shirt that is comfortable and not too tight, shorts or skirt, socks, shoes and a sweater or a tracksuit. Absorbant cotton clothing is best to cope with perspiration.

Shoes

Tennis shoes are probably the most important item of clothing as it is no fun trying to run and move quickly in shoes which are uncomfortable or unsuitable for the court surface. Do not purchase shoes that are tight, as your feet will expand when they are warm.

There are four main types of sole: smooth ones for indoor use on carpets etc, and herringbone, ribbed or nubbed pattern soles for outdoor use. As a general guide the more slippery the court the more grip you will need from the sole of the shoe. Avoid the high bumper jogger type shoes which are unsuitable for fast turning and movement and are often banned by the tennis clubs because of the damage they cause to the courts.

Where to play

Now comes the big decision as to where you are going to play. School tennis courts are available to most youngsters in education. Local authority and park courts are normally available to the public on an hourly rental charge. Tennis clubs usually have a private membership and you have to apply to join. In some cases new members have to be proposed and seconded; but if you do not know anybody who is a member most clubs will consider your application and arrange for a meeting with the club secretary prior to acceptance.

Tennis clubs generally offer opportunities for regular play of all standards. The more organized clubs offer coaching, competitions and social events. These should include introductory coaching courses – both individual and group – advanced coaching courses for all ages, plus internal club competitions, such as ladders and leagues etc, culminating in inter-club competitions. The members of a progressive tennis club will find that most of their tennis needs are met within the club framework.

Coaching

If you do have coaching, ensure that your coach has the necessary qualifications. In Great Britain the coaching qualifications are as follows:–
   *LTA Elementary Tennis Teacher who is qualified to teach at beginner level.
   **LTA Assistant Coach. Qualified to coach up to County Junior level.

   ***LTA Professional Tennis Coach who is qualified to teach at all levels.
However, if you are taking lessons remember the tennis coach is not there just to help you solely with technique, he can give you advice on most subjects including training, tactics, competitions, equipment etc.

LTA Coach Sue Mappin training the Junior Squad.

The LTA Beginner Group coaching course at Crystal Palace.

At various centres throughout Britain the LTA organises LTA/Prudential Beginner Group coaching courses during the Spring and Summer months which comprise six one hour lessons. These courses are an ideal introduction to tennis for children and can lead into further opportunities at County, and even regional and national level for the more promising players.

Competitions

For many players the greatest thrill in tennis is the thrill of competition. Here is a chance to test your capabilities against other players in matches, tournaments, etc. There is a whole range of opportunities available which include tournaments organised by schools, clubs, counties, regions, and finally at national level. There are also inter club matches, league matches and ratings tournaments.

Details of these events are normally available from the clubs, county tennis associations or the Lawn Tennis Association. (See page 144).

Well, having chosen your equipment, your court, and your opponent, now it is time to improve your game by studying some of the world's great players in action in the following chapters.

All instructions given in the book refer to right handed players.

'He' has been used throughout the book only for the sake of brevity.

Part One: The basic strokes

Whatever your standard of play there are some basic fundamentals to which you should try to adhere if you aim to be a successful tennis player.

Good stroke technique is based on being in the right place at the right time. There are many different methods of strokeplay, but providing you are well balanced, move well to the ball and understand where the ball and racket should meet on contact point, then you are well on the way to producing a sound, balanced stroke. It is then that your own individual interpret-ation of technique can be effective. Remember, Wimbledon champions do not all strike the ball in the same way, or even use the same method of gripping the racket, but they do keep to the same basic fundamentals.

Having mastered **how** to hit the ball effectively, you can then move on to the more important side of tennis which in-volves **how** to win the match. Technique is never an end in itself, rather the beginning of your tactical strategy.

Requirements for sound, simple hitting

BALL SENSE
If you play a moving ball game it is neces-sary to have what is known as 'ball sense', namely an ability to move well in relation to the ball in order to play an efficient stroke.

HITTING AREA
In tennis you have to apply your ball sense in order to judge the correct hitting area whether you are playing a groundstroke after the ball has bounced once, or taking it before the bounce on a service, volley or smash.

GROUNDSTROKES

In order to 'groove' your forehand and backhand drives, you should allow the ball to travel over the top of the bounce so that you then strike it in a comfortable hitting area between knee and waist. Take your racket back in good time and give yourself room to swing the racket. Keep the ball a comfortable distance to the *side* of you when hitting. Remember to turn your body sideways so that your hitting area is on a line with your leading foot. This allows the weight of your body to transfer into the shot.

Concentrate on **watching the ball** so that you read and understand the flight of the ball. Check that your contact point is at the correct **height**, **width** and **depth**.

Problems and solutions

It is very easy to rush towards the ball and thus strike it too soon. Learn from the good players and by **preparing early** create extra time so that you can wait for the ball rather than rushing in to it.

Practice

Even before using the racket your hitting area can be greatly improved by practising with a partner, throwing the ball to and fro to each other and catching it after one bounce at the correct height, width and depth. You may be surprised how much movement is required to ensure a perfect contact point every time. Successful hitting is based on this simple requirement.

Ivan Lendl in the correct hitting area for drives

THE SERVICE

The placement of the ball is one of the most vital aspects of the service. The three dimensions of your hitting area are all essential.

Height should be a comfortable distance above your head so that your racket arm is at full stretch when you strike the ball.

Width should be slightly to the right hand side of the body.

Depth should be slightly in front of the leading shoulder to allow the body weight to transfer on point of impact.

Problems and solutions

Remember you are 'placing' the ball in the air. Avoid flinging it above you as this will immediately take it off course.

Practice

Good ball placement must be worked at. Use the stop netting as a target and practise the ball placement and the racket action together. This will help the accuracy of your placement and improve your service rhythm.

Boris Becker in the correct hitting area for service

23

VOLLEYS

Volleys are played before the ball has bounced, but again it is important to get the correct contact point.

The **height** of the ball will vary considerably as this will depend on the type of shot your opponent plays to you.

Width is not quite so far to the side as a drive but the contact point should still be *slightly* to the side.

Depth should be as far forward as possible and at least on a line with the leading hip.

Jimmy Connors in the correct hitting area for volleys

Problems and solutions

A poor understanding of the block, punching action used for volleys often leads to a late contact point.

Practice

If you are just beginning to learn the volley try to practise with a partner without using your rackets and again throw a ball from a volleying position some 7–8 feet (2–2½ metres) from the net, catching it with the racket playing hand at the correct contact point. Remember volleys will be struck at varying heights ranging from shoulder height to below knee height so quick movement is essential. Study how the top players bend their knees to reach forward to volley a low ball.

SMASH

The smash is often regarded as the most attacking shot in tennis. The ball should be struck in a similar hitting area to the service. The obvious difference is that for a smash you have not placed the ball in the air yourself so you must move quickly underneath it to get the correct contact point.

Problems and solutions

It is always difficult to move backwards with speed so try to develop a sidestepping movement backwards so that you are on balance when you strike the ball. Try not to allow the ball to go behind you.

Practice

In the early stages again practise moving back quickly to catch a ball which has been thrown high over your head. Try to catch the ball at the top of your reach and in front of you.

The use of the racket head

Once you have improved your reading and understanding of the flight of the ball for all the basic shots, move on to a better use of the racket.

There are three main areas to concentrate on:

The **swinging** action required for groundstrokes.

The **throwing** action required for service and smash.

The short **punching** and **blocking** action for volleys.

THE SWINGING ACTION FOR GROUNDSTROKES

Concentrate on the correct hitting area as this will give you time to groove your swing.

Take your racket back **early** and immediately you see the ball coming towards you. Observe your opponent's hitting area so that you can anticipate where the ball is travelling.

At the beginning of the forward swing keep your racket face perpendicular to the ground and slightly below the height of the ball.

Swing through to contact point level with your leading hip.

Follow through high, still keeping good control of the racket face so that you feel you are hitting **through** the ball.

Ivan Lendl swings the racket head on the forehand drive

THE THROWING ACTION FOR SERVICE AND SMASH

Boris Becker serves

Take your racket back smoothly to a throwing position behind your back.

Bend your elbow so that you feel your racket head is well down your back.

Throw the racket head at the ball, reaching up to your highest hitting point.

Follow through over the top of the ball, allowing the racket to finish on the left side of your body.

THE PUNCHING ACTION FOR VOLLEYS

Jimmy Connors punches the racket head on the forehand volley

Imagine yourself catching a ball in the palm of your hand and then with the racket make exactly the same blocking action.

Keep your wrist firm and the racket head steady so that the ball bounces off the racket rather like a rebound from a wall.

Make a **short forward** movement with the racket, concentrating on the contact point in front and slightly to the side of your body.

Make certain that your racket head remains steady after impact rather than swinging through.

Martina Navratilova punches a high backhand volley

The ready position

Between all shots you should recover to a central ready position between your forehand and backhand drives or volleys. The ready position will help you to keep your wrist firm and the racket head up. It will also enable you to move in any direction. Point the racket head towards the net and put your non-playing hand on the throat of the racket. If you are a two handed player it is advisable to hold your two hands close together on the racket handle.

Keep your feet a comfortable distance apart, your knees slightly bent and your weight slightly forward so that you are on your toes – like a cat about to jump.

When striking the ball your grip should be firm on the racket handle. Between shots in the ready position you should relax your grip slightly and let the racket rest on your non-playing supporting hand.

For groundstrokes your ready position when rallying should be approximately 3–4 feet (1–1½ metres) behind the baseline.

For volleys you need to be some 7–8 feet (2–2½ metres) from the net.

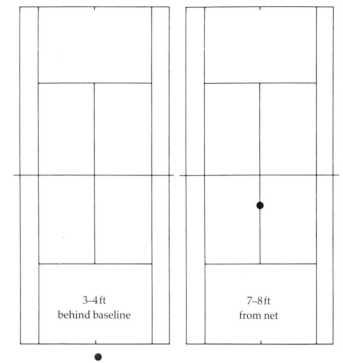

3–4 ft
behind baseline

7–8 ft
from net

Ready position for drives   *Ready position for volleys*

Two top players in the ready position

Basic stroke technique

GROUNDSTROKES

It is usually necessary to change your grip when you play different strokes, but not all tennis players use the same method of gripping. Use grips which are comfortable and compatible with your style of play. Having established them try to keep them consistent. This will help you to develop grooved strokes which should be working as well for you in the final set as when you first start warming up.

The main grips used for forehand drives are the **eastern**, the **western** and the **continental**.

For backhands the more conventional grip for single handed players is the **eastern backhand grip**.

Two handed backhand players may use two forehand grips or may prefer to use an eastern backhand grip with their leading hand and a forehand grip with their lower hand. We strongly recommend that the leading hand, namely the one you serve and play single handed shots with, should be at the butt end of the handle, nearest to the player's body.

For service the most commonly used grip is the 'chopper' continental grip.

For volleys many players use the same grips as on their groundstrokes. Others adopt a halfway point similar to the chopper grip.

The technique and hitting area required for all these grips will be looked at on the following pages through the strokes of the top players. Concentrate on your basic drives first, then we will move on to the more advanced use of spins.

THE EASTERN FOREHAND GRIP

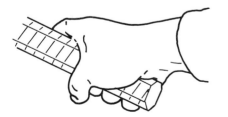

Eastern forehand grip

HOW TO FIND THE EASTERN GRIP
1 Hold the racket at the throat in your non playing hand.
2 Place the palm of your playing hand behind the handle of the racket and wrap your fingers round the handle.
3 Feel as if you are shaking hands with the racket handle. This grip will help you to achieve a firm, flat hit as the palm of the

Jimmy Connors plays a left handed forehand drive

hand behind the handle will give you greater strength. It should also help you to cope more effectively with balls of varying heights.

THE SWING OF THE RACKET
1   Start from the ready position.
2   As the ball travels towards you swing the racket back behind you keeping the racket head perpendicular to the ground and your wrist firm.
3   Pivot your weight back on the right foot as your body turns sideways.
4   Swing the racket towards the ball keeping your arm extended.
5   Contact point should be on a line with your leading hip and a comfortable distance to the side of the body. (Remember **height**, **width** and **depth** required for **hitting area**.)
6   Keep your wrist firm as you follow through. Imagine your racket keeping contact with the ball for as long as possible.

Chris Lloyd bends low for a forehand drive

7 Keep your head down and your eyes on the ball throughout the stroke.
8 Maintain a well balanced position throughout the stroke.
9 Allow your body to pivot so that your shoulders turn towards the net on your follow through.
10 Recover to the ready position.
From the pictures notice how well Chris Lloyd maintains balance throughout the stroke and is able to gain a forward momentum having played the shot.

THE WESTERN FOREHAND GRIP

Western grip

Although the eastern forehand grip is the one most generally used, many players use the western forehand grip which encourages a greater use of top spin.

HOW TO FIND THE WESTERN GRIP

1 Hold the racket at the throat in your non playing hand.
2 Place the palm of your hand underneath the racket handle and wrap your fingers round the handle.
Note: There are variations within the western grip and some players will use a grip half way between eastern and western. Adapt your grip to what suits you best.

THE SWING OF THE RACKET

1 From the ready position swing the racket back early with the racket head low.
2 Keep a more open body stance than for the eastern grip.
3 Swing through to strike the ball well in front of the body.
4 Contact area will be slightly closer to the body as the arm is less extended.
5 The closed racket face achieved with this grip necessitates a more pronounced use of the wrist.
6 The arc of the follow through will be more extreme from low to high.
Notice how Boris Becker, using the western grip, is able to cope with high bouncing balls so effectively. It is also ideal for the forehand drive played from the left side of the court to the right side when running round the backhand.

Boris Becker uses a pronounced western grip

THE CONTINENTAL FOREHAND GRIP

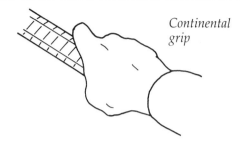

Continental grip

Perhaps one of the most successful players to have used a continental grip was England's Fred Perry. Players introduced to tennis on fast surface courts with a low bounce often find this grip effective. Nowadays, however, more top class tennis is played on slower court surfaces which give a higher bounce and often the continental grip players experience problems under these conditions. This grip is therefore used less and less in modern tennis.

**HOW TO FIND
THE CONTINENTAL GRIP**
1   Hold the racket at the throat in your non playing hand.
2   Place the V between your thumb and forefinger over the top of the handle and wrap your fingers round.

THE SWING OF THE RACKET
1   Preparation is similar to the previous drives but the contact point of racket and ball is slightly behind the leading foot, i.e. **later**.
2   As the contact point is further behind the leading foot there is a greater need for a controlled wrist action.
This grip can be effective when taking the ball on the rise and when slice is used.

THE EASTERN BACKHAND GRIP

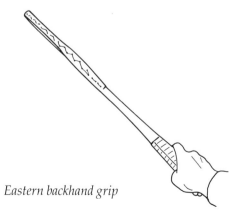

Eastern backhand grip

If you are to be a successful player you must be equally competent on both wings. It is important that you are able to slip quickly and easily into a background grip which will help you play a sound, lifted stroke.

HOW TO FIND THE BACKHAND GRIP
1   Start with eastern forehand grip.
2   Move your hand a quarter of a turn over the top of the handle with your thumb lying diagonally across the back of the handle.

John McEnroe swings through to contact point

3 Slip into this grip as you take your racket back in preparation for the shot.
4 Keep your non playing hand on the racket until you begin your forward swing. This grip gives greater strength behind the handle but gives the player a degree of flexibility.

THE SWING OF THE RACKET
1 Start from a ready position.
2 Take your racket back early with the non playing hand still supporting the throat of the racket.
3 Turn your shoulders as you swing back so that the back of your leading shoulder is pointing towards the net.
4 Keep your racket head low below the height of the ball with the racket face perpendicular to the ground.
5 Swing through with **one hand** on the racket.
6 Contact point should be slightly ahead of the leading foot.
7 Keep your head down on point of impact.
8 Follow through with the racket head finishing high.
9 Feel that you are 'lifting' the ball over the net.

10 Allow your body to turn as you complete the stroke.
Notice in the pictures how well McEnroe and Mandlikova prepare for the shot and keep balanced throughout the stroke, allowing the body weight to transfer into the shot as it is played.
Make certain that the contact point is correct so that your weight can go forward into the shot as you play the stroke.

Hana Mandlikova prepares to hit a backhand

35

THE TWO HANDED BACKHAND GRIP

While players like John McEnroe and Ivan Lendl strike the ball with one hand on the racket, other top players such as Jimmy Connors and Chris Lloyd maintain a two handed grip on the racket. Even within the two handed grip there are variations.

Jimmy Connors keeps two forehand grips on the racket throughout the stroke and very rarely lets go with the non leading hand.

Chris Lloyd slips the leading hand into a backhand grip and on occasions is able to

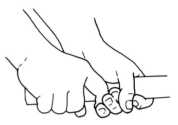

Two views of the two handed backhand grip using a forehand and backhand grip

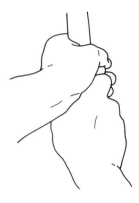

Jimmy Connors keeps two forehand grips on the racket throughout the stroke and copes with a high-bouncing ball

let go with the non leading hand if the situation demands it.

The two handed backhand does help players to put more weight into the shot, but to get into the ideal hitting position it is vitally important to move quickly and well. Two handed players often need to be quicker on their feet to make their stroke a really attacking weapon.

Two handed backhand grip using two forehand grips

HOW TO FIND THE TWO HANDED BACKHAND GRIP

1 Keep your hands close together with your leading hand near the end of the handle.

2 Either keep your two forehand grips, which may mean that you are weak if you have to let go with one hand,

3 Or slip your leading hand into a backhand grip and maintain the lower hand in a forehand grip.

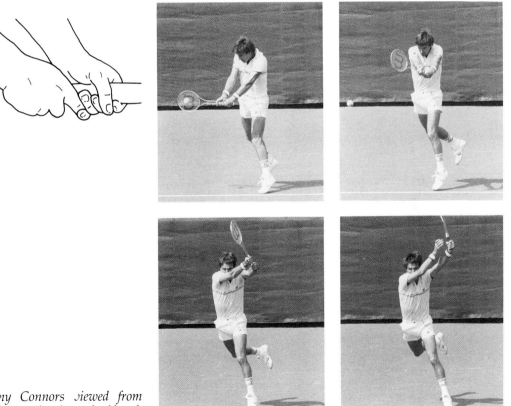

Jimmy Connors viewed from the front as he plays a backhand

Chris Lloyd slips the leading hand into a backhand grip and on occasions is able to let go with the non-leading hand

THE SWING OF THE RACKET

1 Start from a ready position but slip your left hand down the handle so that it is close to your right hand.

2 Swing the racket back early, allowing your shoulders and hips to pivot sideways.

3 Keep the racket head low and the racket face perpendicular to the ground.

4 Swing through to strike the ball, keeping the contact point slightly closer to the body than for a single handed shot as the reach is less.

Again the player is able to let go with the non leading hand

5 Follow through high, allowing your body to pivot round to face the net.

Notice that there is less sideways turn for a two handed backhand but far more body movement as the stroke is played. The pivot of the hips is necessary to get the full body weight into the shot.

Problems and solutions

If you are having problems with your groundstrokes, use this simple checklist to help you eradicate the fault.

1 Is the ball being struck in the correct hitting area in relation to the body?

Note: If your stroke is continually going across your body the ball may be too far in front of you when you strike it. If the ball is too far behind your body, you will lose control of the racket face and the shot will tend to go off to the side. If you feel unable to swing the racket correctly and find that your drive is being pushed beyond the baseline it is likely that the ball is too close to you. Remember the **height**, **width** and **depth** for the correct **hitting area**.

2 Have you moved quickly and well to get into the correct hitting area? If not, why not? Have you failed to move?

3 Have you prepared with an early backswing so that you are well prepared to play your shot?

4 Have you lost control of the racket face by using the incorrect grip?

5 Is the racket swinging effectively through the ball or have you stopped the racket on impact point? This will often

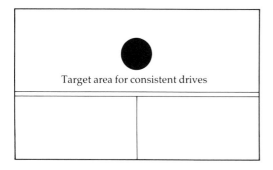

Target areas on the wall

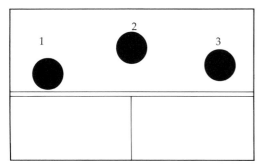

1. Straight backhand target
2. Crosscourt target
3. Straight forehand target

Drive practices

Simple target area for
rally in the service box

result in the ball travelling too high over the net.

6 Have you turned sideways or are you playing the shot with your body square to the net?

7 Have you maintained your balance throughout the stroke?

If you lift your head too soon this will often result in a poor stroke.

Concentrate on directing your swing towards your target area right through the stroke.

Practice

SOLO

1 Use a practice wall, bounce the ball beside you and swing through, concentrating on correct contact point and pathway of racket swing. Count the number of successful hits.

As your control improves consider the following points to add variety to the practice. Otherwise the wall will always tend to beat you!

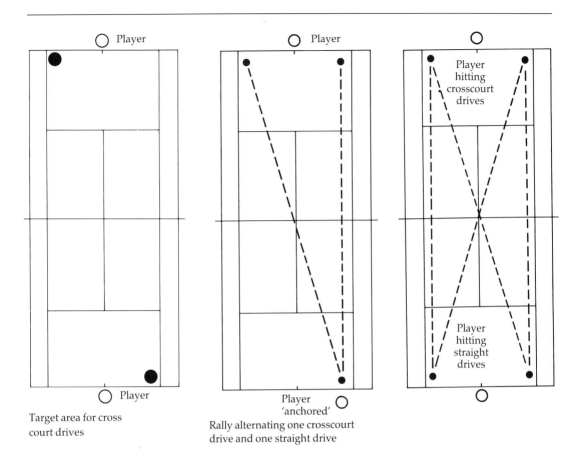

Target area for cross court drives

Rally alternating one crosscourt drive and one straight drive

(a) Give yourself a target area on the wall.
(b) Play a 'pattern' practice, i.e. two forehand drives followed by two backhand drives.
(c) Use target areas on the ground to vary the length and direction of your shots.

PAIRS

1 Get your practice partner to hit balls gently from the net and see if you can hit them to a given target area on the court.

2 Rally with your partner trying to keep the ball in the two forehand service boxes and then repeat for backhand.
3 Try to hit your shots beyond the service box but still in the diagonal of the court.
4 Bring in more movement by recovering to the centre of the court after each shot.
5 Hit straight drives to each other, one player hitting forehand drives near the sideline and the other backhand drives.
6 'Anchor' yourself on the forehand side of the court and play one crosscourt fore-

41

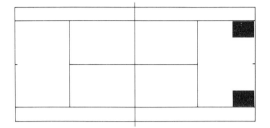

Area where good length drives or volleys should bounce

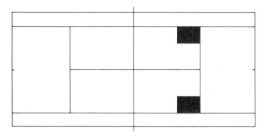

Area where good angled shots should bounce

hand and one straight forehand. Your practice partner will then play one crosscourt forehand and one straight backhand drive. Reverse roles and move on to an anchored backhand position.

Note: This can be a good practice for an average player anchored playing with a stronger player who has to do more running.

7 Finally allow the anchored player to play either crosscourt or straight drives at random and the player under pressure still has to return every shot to the set anchored position.

8 Use a 'running drive' drill where one player hits only crosscourt drives and the other player hits straight drives. First of all see how many shots you can keep going in any one rally and then make it competitive and score a point every time your partner makes a mistake or plays out of sequence.

9 Develop the running drives drill so that either player may hit crosscourt or straight

drives when they wish. Again score points.

10 Play a game in which only drives may be played in the area between the service line and the base line.

Note: It is better to have a rally of twelve shots from inside the service boxes than none outside it. Start all these drills simply and build on your progress. Initially, create time by hitting well above the height of the net and as your control improves try to inject more pace into your drives and hit lower over the net. Remember always that the net is six inches higher at the net posts than at the centre band. Therefore, straight drives near the sidelines must be hit *higher* to clear the net than the safer crosscourt shots hit over the centre of the net.

Try these practice drills and see how your ball control improves. Success makes for *fun*. Success breeds success!

The service

Your service could be your greatest weapon, so spend time on developing this vital stroke in the game. Remember this is the one shot in tennis which your opponent is unable directly to affect so don't rush into it too quickly. Take your time. Start in a well balanced position and in the correct area of the court. In singles, this should be fairly near the centre line. In doubles, stand half way between the centre line and inner sideline so that your court is well covered. Make certain you do not step on to the line with either foot before you have struck the ball as this is a *footfault*.

GRIP

When you first take up the game it is likely that you will serve with the grip you use on your forehand drive. This is acceptable as you develop confidence in your ball placement and your ability to get the ball in the service box. However, to gain a better throwing action with the racket head you should consider adjusting your grip to the chopper grip as this will give you more flexibility in the wrist and thus more throwing power in the racket head.

The chopper grip is half way between the eastern forehand and the eastern backhand grip. The V of the thumb and forefinger should be placed over the top of the racket handle with your fingers spread comfortably around the handle. Allow your index finger to spread out slightly more to give a flexible grip which will help your wrist action.

STANCE

Start in a good throwing position with your body turned sideways to the net, your feet comfortably astride and your body weight evenly distributed.

Point the racket in the direction you wish to serve and allow the ball to rest on the throat of the racket.

BALL PLACEMENT

As you begin to take your racket back, place the ball in the air with your left hand. Concentrate on the contact point already mentioned, namely to a comfortable height slightly to the side and slightly in front of your leading shoulder.

RACKET THROW

As the ball is placed in the air, take your racket back in a smooth, rhythmical move to behind your back. Notice the powerful throwing stance of Navratilova (pages 46–7) as the racket is poised to throw at the ball. Even if both feet are off the ground on the point of impact balance is maintained, but develop a sound action before you progress to this advanced move.

RACKET HEAD CONTROL

When you first use a chopper grip you may find that you have difficulty in getting the ball in the service box and that it slices too far over to your left. This is because you are not opening your wrist and thus not allowing the racket face to brush across the ball. In the early stages imagine you are serving to a target area much farther to

Boris Becker serves viewed from the side

your right hand side than usual and think of your racket meeting the ball square on. Try to strike the ball at the top of your reach and then bring the racket head over the ball and down to finish on the left hand side of your body.

BALANCE
To develop the correct throwing action you may find that it helps to start with the racket in the throwing position behind your back. Place the ball in the air and gently throw the racket head at it, feeling your wrist action. As this improves add on the full service action and bring in more of your own body weight into the serve. Just

as with a normal throwing action, start with your weight on the back foot and allow it to transfer forward to the front foot as you strike the ball.

Problems and solutions

BALL PLACEMENT
Poor placement of the ball can lead to most of the problems encountered in the service.
If you place the ball too low, your contact point will be incorrect and you will push the racket head at the ball and hit the ball out. If the ball is too far forward you may

be tempted to take a step towards it and then find that you are off balance as you hit, resulting in a service into the net.

If the ball is too far back your body weight has no chance to transfer forward and the service will lack power and direction and will probably go out beyond the service box.

SERVICE RHYTHM

Some players find great difficulty in working the ball and racket together in unison. If you experience difficulties start the racket and ball together but then start moving the racket downwards before you place the ball in the air. This will allow the hands to separate and go naturally in their opposite directions. As you place the ball in the air feel as if your left arm is reaching upwards to keep contact with the ball for as long as possible. This should help with both direction and balance.

BODY POSITION

If you have problems keeping your feet balanced on the ground when serving put a ball box or a racket headcover on your feet to remind you to keep them firmly anchored to the ground. Players are often tempted to move because the ball placement is too far forward.

Martina Navratilova in the service throwing action

Practice

1 Improve your basic throwing action by throwing balls overarm over the net. Concentrate on the correct sideways throwing stance and transfer of body weight. As you improve try to increase your accuracy and power.

2 Practise your ball placement as you take your racket back into the throwing position. Work on getting the ball and racket to work in unison.

3 Practise serves to target areas in the services boxes:

(a) to the corner of the box,

(b) down the centre service line,

(c) down the middle of the service box,

(d) as a shorter, wider angle half way down the sideline.

4 Serve to a partner who will return your service.

5 Serve and play the rally out.

Note: While solo practice is essential it is also important to practise serving to an opponent and to play your next shot, either as a drive or ultimately as a volley. Also always remember to practise the service to both the right and the left service box! Often the thought of recovering for the rally will upset your balance and the service suffers. Not all your serves will be aces no matter how long you practise, so be ready for that next shot.

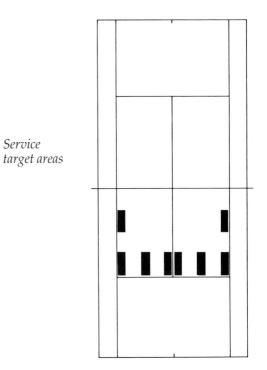

Service target areas

Net play

If you have developed a sound attacking service and are competent on your groundstrokes you should have plenty of opportunity to make attacking moves forward to the net. You need to advance from a sound base as this will make your net play easier.

Martina Navratilova at full stretch

POSITIONING

The only time you start at the net is when your partner is serving in doubles. On every other occasion you must make the move forwards and this means that many volleys will be played as low volleys from the mid court area. Providing these are played to a good depth you should then be able to move closer to the net to finish the rally off with an attacking volley or smash. In the early stages when you are developing your confidence at the net, it is advisable to take up a position some 7–8 feet (2–2½ metres) from the net and practise your volleys from there. Even at this distance you may have to cope with balls of varying height.

THE FOREHAND VOLLEY

Pam Shriver strikes the ball well forward

GRIP

Try to use either the eastern forehand grip or the continental grip for your volley, rather than a western forehand grip, as this tends to close the racket face and makes the low volley a particular problem.

USE OF THE RACKET HEAD

Start from a ready position and block or punch your racket towards the ball, trying to hit it slightly to the side of you but well forward. Open the racket face *slightly* to give you greater control. Notice how the shoulders turn slightly sideways and the leading foot steps forward into the shot. Keep to a short action and avoid too much forward swing on the follow through. The volley is esentially a *short*, *quick* action. Recover immediately to a ready position so that you are prepared for the next shot.

THE BACKHAND VOLLEY

GRIP
Use the eastern backhand grip as this will give you extra strength. If your wrist is strong enough use the continental grip and then you will not have to make a grip change between the two volleys. This will often be an advantage in a quick exchange of shots at the net, providing you are able to keep your racket head steady.

USE OF THE RACKET HEAD
Start in a ready position with your racket supported at the throat in your non-playing hand. Block or punch forward to strike the ball slightly to the side and well in front of you. Avoid swinging the racket head at the ball. If there is time step forward on your leading foot to put weight into the shot.

Kathy Jordan uses the western grip for the backhand volley. Not an easy shot!

Martina Navratilova maintains balance at the net

John McEnroe in a well balanced position to play a backhand volley

THE TWO HANDED BACKHAND VOLLEY

Jimmy Connors copes with a low two handed volley

Players who use two hands for their back-hand drives often continue with the two handed backhand at the net. Even then there are occasions when they are stretched wide and this is when the single handed backhand volley will be of more use.

GRIP
As for the groundstrokes it is advisable to slip the leading hand into a more pro-nounced eastern backhand grip so that you are able to let go with the supporting hand should the need arise. Again the two hands should be placed close together on the handle.

USE OF THE RACKET HEAD
For the low volley it is still essential for the two handed player to punch or block at the ball, taking it to the side but not quite as far forward as for the single handed shot.

For the higher ball, the two handed back-hand can be an extremely effective shot if played as a drive volley, i.e. a powerful attacking volley played with more swing.

Problems and solutions

Too much swing of the racket head is a major cause of problems on all volleys. A swinging preparation leads to a late impact point.
Keep to the short forward blocking action.
Slow movement at the net can result in a rushed shot. You have less time to react to the ball when at the net. Keep on your toes and be ready to pounce forward into your volley.
A loose grip will result in loss of control of the racket head and your volley will lack firmness and placement. Whatever your method of gripping, keep your grip and

53

wrist firm and feel that your racket is a solid wall from which the ball will rebound.

If you have difficulty controlling the ball open the racket face slightly to put a little underspin on the ball. But on very high volleys hit with the racket face slightly closed. If you are caught out on the lower balls remember to bend your knees to get down to them. Again open the racket face but keep your wrist firm.

Practice

SOLO

1 Stand 7–8 feet (2–2½ metres) from a practice wall and gently tap the ball against the wall. Keep your wrist firm and allow hardly any movement in the racket head. This will strengthen your forearm and improve your blocking action.

2 Set up a variety of practice sequences that will encourage control and variety of volleys. Give yourself target areas and use a pattern practice as already outlined for drives, i.e. ten forehand volleys, ten backhand volleys, followed by two forehand volleys and two backhand volleys.

PAIRS

1 Stand in the ready position at the net and get a partner to throw balls to you so that you can volley to a target area. Practise both forehand and backhand volleys, recovering to the ready position after each shot.

2 Get your partner to drive the ball to you and again volley it back to a given target area. Remember you should get into the habit of volleying the ball away from your opponent, so put your targets in the corners of the court near the baseline and near the service line. Practise both cross-court and straight volleys.

3 For a continuous exercise anchor your partner in one area of the court and volley every shot back to that target area. This should increase your movement.

4 Set up an exercise where both you and your partner are volleying. This shows you how quick your movement must be and why it is so necessary to keep a short blocking action. You should soon discover that there is no time to swing your racket.

5 Play a conditioned game where both players start on the service line. Set the ball up in the service box and move forward with the aim of trying to win the point with a volley. To begin with make a rule that all volleys must be no deeper than the service box but as you improve develop this to include the whole court.

THE SMASH

If you advance to the net and put your opponent under pressure it is very likely that he or she will try to remove you from this attacking position by lobbing the ball high over your head in the hope that you will have to retreat to the back of the court. Try not to give up your attacking position and rather than being forced to run backwards try to take the ball when it is in the air on your smash. If played well this should be the ultimate attacking shot. Similar to the service action the racket head should be thrown *aggressively* at the ball.

GRIP

Hold the racket in the grip you use for your service, hopefully by now the chopper grip.

POSITION

You are likely to be lobbed when you are near the net and if your opponent manages to play a high lob it will be necessary for you to move back quickly in order to smash. From the ready position at the net turn and move backwards, using a sidestepping action in order to keep your balance.

USE OF THE RACKET HEAD

Keep the ball in front of you and as you take your racket back to a throwing position behind your head, point up at the ball with your non playing hand. This will help to get your shoulders round sideways and will aid your balance. Throw the racket head at the ball concentrating on a contact point slightly in front and to the side of you, similar to the service contact point.

Hit the ball at the highest point of your reach, allowing your weight to come forward as you strike the ball. Bring the racket head through as you would for service.

Problems and solutions

Poor positioning in relation to the ball is the major problem to affect the smash. Concentrate on the correct contact point and practise your movement backwards. Players who try to run backwards quickly while still facing the net and looking up at the lob stand a great risk of falling over backwards! Poor backward movement may also result in a poor hitting area and it is then particularly difficult to control the shot.

Practice

SOLO

1 If you can use a high practice wall, stand some 7–8 feet (2–2½ metres) from it and smash the ball on the ground before the wall so that it rebounds up on to the wall and then travels above your head. Move quickly and smash it down on the ground again and it should rebound for you to smash again, and again. This is not an easy exercise but is especially good to speed up your racket preparation, wrist action and footwork. Start gently and count the number of successful hits. As your control and confidence improve you can start to use more power.

Martina Navratilova displays the balanced hitting position required for the smash

PAIRS

1 With a partner practise lobs and smashes. As for all the previous strokes practise smashing to a target area in the corners of the court. Always try to recover to your volley ready position.

2 Practise a volley and then a smash. This should encourage you to play an attacking volley and then move in to put the ball away as a winning smash.

The lob

This is a shot which should never be underrated, whether used in singles or doubles. A lob can be used to force an aggressive net player away from an attacking position at the net. A lob will also create recovery time if you are under pressure at the back of the court. It may also set up an attacking move from a seemingly defensive position.

Notice the open racket face and long follow through on this backhand lob played by Hana Mandlikova

THE FOREHAND LOB

GRIP
This should be similar to the grip used for the basic forehand drive.

USE OF THE RACKET HEAD
Again a swinging racket head is necessary. Prepare as quickly as possible. Remember that often a lob has to be played when under pressure so it is *essential* to get the racket back as quickly as possible. Start the racket head low, open the racket face and hit up positively under the ball. Follow through, trying to imagine that you are keeping contact with the ball for as long as possible to give you greater control.

THE BACKHAND LOB

GRIP
Again use a similar grip to your basic drive whether you use a single handed backhand or two handed.

USE OF THE RACKET HEAD
Prepare early and open the racket face to hit underneath the ball. The contact point should be slightly ahead of the leading foot. Concentrate on a long follow through.

Problems and solutions

You may find that you do not have time to get in to a good hitting position. You must still try to maintain good balance by pivoting your shoulders sideways.

Late racket preparation will lead to a late contact point which makes control of the racket head difficult. Prepare the racket early.

Lack of height on the lob could have been caused by a failure to open the racket face and hit up through the ball.

Practice

1　Use the drills already outlined for forehand and backhand drives but play lobs instead. Try to get your lob to bounce near the baseline.

Again the use of the backhand lob when the player (Stefan Edburg) is under pressure.

Tactics

Having looked at the technique required for sound, simple strokeplay, let us now look at the tactical side of the game when your repertoire of strokes can be put to good use.

SINGLES TACTICS

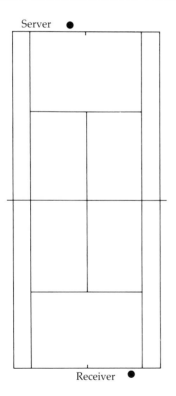

Server

Receiver

In order to be able to play balanced strokes and keep your opponent on the move, try to keep to the following simple match tactics which apply whatever your level of play.

Singles court position

1 Start in a good position on the court. This means serving from approximately a foot from the centre mark and then moving immediately to just behind the baseline in the centre of the court.

2 Remember your ready position. Keep your weight on the balls of your feet so that you are ready to move off quickly in any direction.

3 Make every effort to reach *every* ball and try to keep your shots within the boundary of the singles court.

4 Try to direct your shots away from the centre of the court as this should make your opponent run and will give him less time to play his shots.

5 Try to wrong-foot your opponent.

6 Observe your opponent carefully, notice his physique, his ability to move well, whether he is right or left handed and his strengths and weaknesses.

7 Try to play to his weaknesses and exploit his strengths by making every effort to retrieve the so-called winning shots.

8 Move to the net when you have the right opportunity to do so. Don't rush forward from a position right at the back of the court. Wait for a ball hit near the ser-

vice line, try to play your shot deep into your opponent's corner of the court and then move forward to the net.

9 Take your time when serving, and again try to place your service so that it tests your opponent's ability to return the ball.

10 Take into account the court and weather conditions and try to use these to your tactical advantage.

11 Remember to keep a positive mental approach. Concentrate on all the points already mentioned and try to develop the patience to keep the ball in play.

12 Above all remember that tennis tactics should be simple:
(a) Ball must go over net
(b) Ball must go into court
(c) Ball must go away from opponent
(d) Ball must be hit forcefully
Too many players fail at tennis matchplay because they try to make (d) their main tactic before doing (a), (b) and (c).
You must practise to be a **winner**! Get your tennis alphabet in the right order.

DOUBLES TACTICS

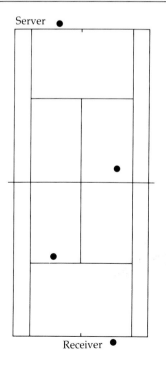

Server

Receiver

The strokeplay required in doubles is obviously the same as in the singles game. However, you now have a partner who is there to work with you to cover the court well. It is, therefore, essential to work as a *team* rather than as two individuals who happen to be on the same side of the net. Again concentrate on the following simple doubles tactics.

1 Start in a good position on the court. Each player should be responsible for half the court but you now have to decide who is going to cope with the balls which travel down the centre of the court. This is often a problem area in doubles. Assuming both players are right handed, it is generally accepted that the player taking the backhand court will move across and take the forehands down the middle of the court.

Doubles court positions at the start of the game

Start in a good position on the court

2 Maintain a good position during the rally. If your partner is pulled out to one side of the court move across to cover the central area. You should feel as if you and your partner are joined together by a piece of string and if one player is pulled in one direction the partner should go across in the same direction to cover the gap.

3 If serving stand half way between the centre line and the inner sideline with your partner at the net ready to intercept on the volley.

4 If receiving the service you should stand just behind the baseline opposite the service box. Your partner should stand just inside the service line ready to move forward to the net if you play a good return of service.

5 The most attacking doubles position is to have both players at the net, but within a rally you may find that both teams have to move forward and backward as the play develops.

6 Try to be aware of where your partner is on the court and be ready to move quickly forward or backward as the need arises.

7 You may possibly not hit one ball in a rally but by covering and moving well you may have influenced the outcome of the rally.

8 The service should be a particular advantage in doubles. If you can force a weak return of service through your powerful delivery, your partner should have the opportunity to intercept and play a winning volley.

9 As in singles observe your opponents carefully. Look for their strengths and weaknesses and try to expose them, but in general play on the weaker partner.

10 As the court is now wider put your

crosscourt shots to good use and try to move the opponents wide so that you test their ability to cover the court well.

As in singles, keep your tactics simple and within your ability to keep to the a, b, c and d of tactics.

Both teams may have to move forwards and backwards as the play develops

Part Two: The use of spin

Once you have developed confidence in your basic stroke technique and have begun to put your tactics into operation, you can start to add variety to your game by using spin on your shots.

Spin on the ball has a number of advantages. First it should help you to control the ball better, particularly in adverse weather conditions. Used on the service it can help you to place the ball with greater safety and precision. Overall it should add control to your game, while making it more difficult for your opponent to cope with your shots.

The types of spin to use

In simple terms there are two main types of spin, topspin and slice. Let us take a look at how they work.

TOPSPIN DRIVES

To impart topspin try to hit **up** and **over** the ball. This will accelerate the movement of the ball as it travels through the air and consequently 'kicks' forward on its impact with the court. This produces a higher and faster bouncing ball for the opponent to return. The topspin pushes the ball downwards so therefore it can be hit higher over the net to increase the safety margin.

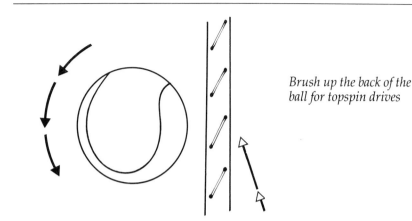

Brush up the back of the ball for topspin drives

TOPSPIN KICK SERVICE

To impart topspin on the service you need to hit **up** and **across** the ball. This will give the ball a higher trajectory over the net but will accelerate the movement of the ball through the air so that it will kick forward on its impact with the court.

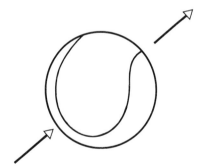

Hit across the ball from the 8 o'clock to 2 o'clock positions for the kick serve

SLICE OR UNDERSPIN DRIVES

For this spin you need to hit **down** and **under** the ball. This generally makes the ball travel more slowly through the air. The ball will revolve in the opposite direction to topspin so that as it makes contact with the ground it keeps the bounce low and reduces the forward propulsion of the ball. The underspin pushes the ball upwards so therefore it needs to be hit closer to the net than for flat drives.

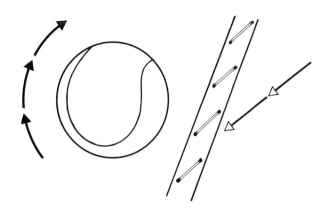

Brush down the back of the ball for slice drives

SLICE OR SIDESPIN SERVICE

For this spin you need to hit approximately level and **round the side** of the ball. This will swerve the ball either out to the side, taking the receiver further out of position to receive the service, or alternatively could swerve the ball into the body of the opponent. Both serves can be difficult to cope with.

SIDESPIN DRIVES

Sidespin may also be used on a shot played close to the body, particularly on a backhand down the line approach shot which could have both slice and sidespin to make it fade away from the opponent.

How to put spin on the ball

OPEN AND CLOSED RACKET FACE

Just as a golfer has a set of clubs all shaped at different angles to cope with the type of shot to be played, so a tennis player needs to adjust the angle of the racket face in order to be able to play the shot selected. The only problem is that in tennis your *one* racket has to do everything for all shots!

For basic strokes we have already stressed that it is effective to keep the racket head perpendicular to the ground on impact point so that you are able to feel that you are hitting firmly through the ball. To impart spin you need to adjust the angle of the racket face.

Use a slightly more closed racket face after imparting topspin and a slightly more open racket face to impart slice. You close the racket by turning the head of the racket so that the hitting face is tilted slightly more towards the ground after impact. To open the racket you turn the head of the racket so that the hitting face is tilted upwards.

(F)   Open racket face

(G)   Closed racket face

When to use spin

Spin can be used on all your shots but particularly on groundstrokes and service. Try to introduce it on these strokes first and then move on to the more advanced shots as your control improves.

Some players will automatically use spin through their method of gripping the racket. Western grip players will favour the use of topspin as this grip tends to encourage a brushing action with the racket face. Players who use a two handed backhand will also tend to use more topspin. Borg and Wilander are good examples of top players who use this method of hitting although obviously they sometimes employ slice as well.

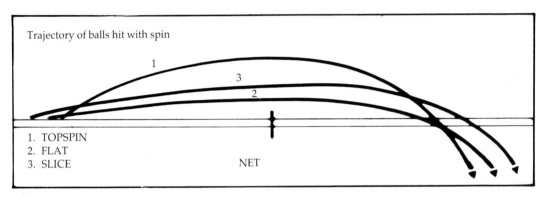

Trajectory of balls hit with spin

1. TOPSPIN
2. FLAT
3. SLICE

NET

TOPSPIN

Gives a higher trajectory over the net and consequently allows more margin for error when hitting aggressively or defensively from any part of the court. Notice the differing trajectories of the ball when hitting flat drives, topspin drives and slice.

The higher bounce may cause problems for the opponent, particularly those who employ a more continental type of grip and who do not like dealing with balls above waist height. The kick forward of the ball also allows more increased angles to be played, particularly useful when playing doubles. A shorter topspin shot can be especially effective against an incoming volleyer who will then have to cope with a more difficult ball dipping down at the feet.

SLICE

This is an effective spin to use in defensive play. It enables you to cope with balls of varying heights more effectively and can allow better control of the ball in certain windy conditions. As slice will tend to keep the ball low it is an effective spin to employ on slow and damp courts. It is also especially effective on an approach shot to the net when you need to take the ball early but need the slice to control the ball.

Players who use the more conventional method of gripping the racket, namely the eastern grip, will often find it easier to employ slice. Generally it is difficult to hit slice drives *aggressively* into court. They must be played with care and the emphasis should be on good placement of the shot.

Compare the difference between *flat, slice* and *topspin* drives.

Assumption: Three balls are hit at 60 mph one foot high over the net.

1   The *flat lifted* drive will land on the baseline.

2   The *sliced* ball will land beyond the base line, so to keep it in court it will have to be hit less aggressively or lower over the net.

3   The *topspin* shot will land near the service line but will kick forward so that the opponent will still be returning the ball from the base line.

Therefore, the topspin shot gives you more safety as the ball can clear the net by a greater margin but can still be hit aggressively and land in the court. Both slice and topspin should be introduced on your service once you have mastered the chopper grip.

How to put spin on your groundstrokes

THE TOPSPIN FOREHAND DRIVE

1 Start from the ready position using the *grip* you would *normally* employ for your basic forehand.
2 Take your *racket back early*, allowing the racket head to *drop lower* than the striking height of the ball. *Swing* through to *contact point* on a line with your leading foot.
3 *Brush* the racket face *up and forward* against the ball.

4 Allow a *controlled wrist action* over the back of the ball as you follow through. This will encourage better *racket head speed*.
5 Feel that the racket head is travelling from **low** to **high** in a more extreme arc than for your basic drive.
6 Keep the racket face *vertical* throughout the shot *closing* on follow through.

Ivan Lendl puts topspin on the forehand drive

Boris Becker allows the racket head to travel from low to high with controlled wrist action and a more pronounced western grip

THE TOPSPIN BACKHAND DRIVE

1 Start from a ready position and as you take your racket back slip into your *normal grip*.
2 Keep the racket head *low on backswing* and the racket face vertical to the ground.
3 Swing through to ball *contact point* slightly ahead of your leading foot.
4 *Brush* vigorously up and forward against the back of the ball.
5 Feel that the racket head is travelling from *low* to *high* in a more extreme arc than for your basic drive.
6 Allow a *controlled* use of *wrist*.
Note: A topspin backhand requires a firm wrist and a very definite eastern backhand grip to allow the racket face to brush the ball firmly. Players often find more difficulty in putting topspin on their backhand because of the lack of strength in the back of the hand.

Boris Becker imparts topspin on the backhand drive

THE TWO HANDED TOPSPIN BACKHAND DRIVE

As we have already seen, the two handed backhand is especially effective for topspin as the strength of the two handed grip often allows for a more vigorous use of the racket face on the ball.

1 Start from a ready position and as you take your racket back try to slip your leading hand into the *eastern backhand grip*. This will help you to *brush* up the back of the ball more effectively. Players who employ two forehand grips all the time, such as Jimmy Connors, tend to use less topspin.

2 Keep the racket head *low* on backswing.

3 Swing through to ball *contact point* just behind the leading foot, i.e. a *slightly* later impact than for the single handed backhand.

4 *Brush* vigorously *up* and *forward* against the back of the ball.

5 Swing the racket head from *low* to *high* in a more extreme arc than for the basic drive.

6 Let the racket face *close* on follow through.

Problems and solutions

1 In the early stages you may find that you are *closing* the racket face too much and are only hitting *over* the top of the ball rather than *up* the back of the ball.

2 Make certain that you concentrate on a good *contact point*. A *late* contact with the ball will encourage a wristy, uncontrolled use of spin.

3 Remember you need a *controlled* wrist action. Avoid using your wrist too much. Over-use of the wrist will encourage a 'flicky' light-weight spin. Your drives still need penetration so remember to hit *up the back of the ball and forward* to gain that extra momentum.

4 If you find that you are unable to get the feeling of brushing up the back of the ball, try to over-emphasize the low racket head preparation and make a very definite move to finish with the racket high, rather as if you were about to play a lob. Be aware of swinging forwards but lead with the *top edge* of the racket going upwards.

5 Always go for good height over the net. Players who use an excessive amount of topspin successfully should never have any fears of not being able to get the ball over the net, as the height at which the ball clears the net could be at least three feet (1 metre) above the net band.

Practice

Use the drills for basic drives but pay particular attention to where the ball lands in the opponent's court. Balls hit with heavy topspin need not be hit as near the baseline as a flat drive as the spin should project the ball onwards so that the opponent still has to cope with a return well behind his baseline. Therefore *you* gain a *greater margin for error*.

THE TOPSPIN SERVICE

Topspin can be particularly useful on the second service as the higher trajectory of the ball clearing the net gives you a safer second service which can still present great problems for your opponent. It may also allow you more time to move to the net if you wish to after your service.

1 Stand in your normal service position using the *chopper grip.*

2 Place the *ball* rather more to the *left* side of your body and less forward than for the basic service.

3 Bring your racket back to the normal throwing position behind your back but allow your *back to arch.*

4 Throw the racket head at the ball bringing the racket face vigorously *up, across and over* the ball.

5 It is essential to develop a good *wrist action* often referred to as *wrist snap* to achieve this *upward brushing* movement.

6 Allow the racket head to finish on the *left* side of the body as for the basic service.

Problems and solutions

1 Inability to achieve topspin even though you have altered your ball placement is often a problem at first, when players find they are still slicing the ball. Try to pay particular attention to the movement of the racket face *up, across and over* the back of the ball. Imagine a clock face and feel that your racket is travelling from eight to two on the clock face.

2 Sometimes players feel that by over exaggerating the ball placement to behind and to the left of the body they will achieve a greater spin. *This is not the case.* Spin is

achieved by a good *wrist action* and an extreme ball placement will only result in an unbalanced and erratic service. There is a saying in tennis that you are only as good as your second service, i.e. if you are unable to get the second serve in consistently, your opponent is gaining an advantage without having to earn it. Make your opponent play the ball and try to get that second service in whenever you play it.

Practice

Use the exercises for the basic service, using set target areas within the service boxes. When moving on to practising with a receiver, first use only your second serve and see how successful you are. Then use your second service as normal when you have missed your first serve. This is more realistic but more difficult because of the different actions being used. It is always best to practise leading up to the sequences of serves which you may use in a match.

Notice John McEnroe's wrist action as the racket is brushed across and over the ball

THE TOPSPIN LOB

Topspin can be particularly effective on a lob. Nothing can be more frustrating for the opponent than to be unable to smash a ball and then have to run backwards quickly in order to retrieve it, only to find that on impact with the court it shoots away for a winner. The topspin lob contains a strong element of surprise. It is a difficult shot to smash and may quickly change a defensive situation into attack by removing the opposition from the net.

THE TOPSPIN FOREHAND LOB

1 Use your *basic grip* but if you do not already use a western grip a *slight* change towards western may help you to get a heavier spin.
2 Prepare as for a normal topspin drive with the racket head well *below* the striking *height of the ball*.
3 Use a hard *brushing action up* the back of the ball with a controlled wrist action *up and over* the back of the ball.
4 Finish with the *racket head high* but the *racket face closed*.
5 Feel the exaggerated low to high movement of the racket.

THE TOPSPIN BACKHAND LOB

1 Use a *similar grip* to the *basic drive*.
2 Prepare early, keeping the *racket head* well *below* the striking height of the ball.
3 Concentrate on meeting the ball in *front* of the leading foot and bring the racket face *up* the back of the ball with a *hard* brushing action.
4 Keep the racket face *closed* but follow through *high*.
5 Feel the exaggerated low to high movement of the racket.

THE TWO HANDED TOPSPIN BACKHAND LOB

1 Use similar grips as for the basic drive but it is advisable to let your leading hand slip into the *eastern backhand grip* as it is likely that on a lob you will need a *long follow through* which is easier if you let go with the left hand. If you use the eastern backhand grip it will help you to *close* the *racket face* during the *follow through*.
2 *Prepare early*, keeping the racket head well *below* the striking height of the ball.
3 *Strike* the ball as far *forward* as possible and bring the racket face *up the back of the ball* with a *hard brushing* action.
4 Follow through high.
5 Feel the exaggerated low to high movement of the racket.

Problems and solutions

If you are to gain a tactical advantage from the topspin lob it is essential to take the ball early. Problems will occur if the contact point is late as you may then be forced into an over-use of the wrist which could cause the ball to drop too short and too low.

Practice

Use the practice drills for the basic lob. Extend the lobbing practices and get your partner to volley at the net. Having played two drives see if on the third shot you are able to play a topspin lob. If it is effective, the net player should be unable to smash it.

THE TOPSPIN SMASH

Tactically, it is obviously advisable to try to maintain control of the net position once you have got there. However, this is not always possible, particularly if the opponent has an effective lob. The *topspin smash* may come into action in this situation. If a ball has been lobbed over your head towards your backhand side it may be possible to smash the ball even though it is not well in front of you, providing you use topspin.

1 Use your basic *service chopper grip.*
2 Take the racket back quickly to a *throwing position* and throw the racket face *up, across and over the ball* in a similar wrist snap action you would use for the topspin service.
3 By giving your smash a *slightly higher trajectory* over the net to the normal more aggressive smash, you should have more time to recover having played your shot.
4 Allow the racket to finish over towards your left side.

Problems and solutions

As the ball is likely to be struck behind your head and sometimes well to the left side, it is essential to maintain balance and get a good wrist snap throwing action. Poor movement backwards, late racket preparation and a poor throwing action are the main causes of failure on a topspin smash.

Practice

Stand in the normal ready position at the net and get your partner to lob a ball diagonally across the court towards the backhand corner so that you have to play a smash from behind your head. Bring in a routine where you play first a volley and then a smash. Finally bring in a random practice where the lob can be played at any time. This will keep the net player on his toes and should put him under the kind of pressure experienced in a match.

79

Slice

THE SLICE FOREHAND DRIVE

1 Start from the ready position using your *normal grip*. Western grip players may like to try slipping the hand into the eastern forehand grip, or possibly the continental grip, which may help them to play a slice forehand more easily.

2 Take your racket back *early* but higher than the striking height of the ball.

3 On the forward swing, keep the racket face *slightly open* and hit *down and through the ball*.

4 Keep your wrist *firm* and allow your body weight to go *forwards* into the shot.

5 Try to imagine keeping a *long contact* with the ball to maintain control.

6 The racket face should remain *open* on follow through.

Zina Garrison slicing a forehand drive

THE SLICE BACKHAND DRIVE

1 Start from the ready position using your *normal backhand grip*.
2 Take the racket back *early* but *higher* than the *striking* height of the ball.
3 Hit *down and through* the ball, keeping the racket face slightly open to give underspin to the ball.

4 Keep a *firm wrist* and allow your body weight to go forwards into the shot.
5 Try to imagine keeping a *long contact* with the ball to maintain control.
6 The racket face should remain *open* on the *follow through*.

Pam Shriver moves from the ready position to play a slice backhand drive

The use of spin

Boris Becker plays an attacking slice backhand allowing his body weight to transfer well forward into the shot

THE SLICE TWO HANDED BACKHAND DRIVE

Two handed players often find slice a more difficult spin to use and favour top-spin unless under extreme pressure, when a defensive shot *has* to be played.

1 Start from the ready position using your *normal backhand grips* but try to use an eastern backhand grip with the leading hand to enable a one handed follow through if extra reach is required.

2 Prepare early as for a normal backhand but allow the racket head to start *higher* than the striking height of the ball as you start your *forward swing*.

3 Hit *down and through* the ball with racket face *slightly open* giving underspin to the ball.

4 Keep a *firm wrist* and allow your *body weight* to go *forwards* into the shot.

5 Imagine keeping a *long contact* with the ball to maintain control.

6 The racket face should *remain* open on the follow through.

Jimmy Connors stretches to play a high back-hand with slice

Problems and solutions

Shots played with slice may have a slightly later impact point than basic drives. However, if you strike the ball too late you will have difficulty controlling the ball and may find that you are tempted to flick the wrist. Try to play the ball in good time. Keep your wrist firm. It is nearly always better to be early on impact rather than late. If you find that your shot is travelling over the net too high, then you are probably hitting under the ball too much, rather than down the back of the ball. Remember to keep the racket face *slightly* open at impact.

Practice

Use the drills already mentioned for basic drives. Once your slice has become well grooved, use the shot as an approach drive and move forward to the net. Slice will add to your control and should keep the bounce of the ball low. The opponent may then be forced to hit higher than he would like, giving you an easy ball to volley. Work with a partner who practises his *top-spin* drives while you practise the *slice* return and then exchange roles. Slice is often a very effective shot to use against a high-bouncing ball, as it will help you to bring the ball down even though you may have been forced to cope with a contact point well above your normal *comfortable hitting area*.

DROPSHOTS

Dropshots should be played with slice and practised as part of the basic drive sequences. They need a delicate touch with backspin on the ball. They are particularly effective against players who are slow moving forward and reluctant to come to the net.

Eventually they should be played with disguise.

Two handed and western grip players may have some difficulty playing dropshots with slice, but it is worth adjusting your grip to develop the use of this shot.

THE FOREHAND DROPSHOT

1   Start from the ready position using your normal grip.
2   Shape up for the stroke as if about to play a drive.
3   Concentrate on a hitting area on a line with the leading foot.
4   Stroke the racket face down the back and underneath the ball.
5   Take the speed off the ball by slowing down the head of the racket on the follow through.
6   Watch the ball carefully and maintain balance throughout the stroke.

THE BACKHAND DROPSHOT

1   Start from the ready position using your normal grip.
2   Shape up for the stroke as if about to play a drive.
3   Concentrate on a hitting area on a line with the leading foot.
4   Stroke the racket face down the back and underneath the ball.
5   Take the speed off the ball by slowing down the head of the racket on the follow through.

6   Watch the ball carefully and maintain balance throughout the stroke.

THE TWO HANDED BACKHAND DROPSHOT

1   Start from the ready position using your normal grip.
2   Shape up for the stroke as if about to play a drive.
3   Concentrate on a hitting area on a line with the leading foot but slightly closer to the body than for the single handed shot.
4   Stroke the racket face down the back and underneath the ball.
5   Take the speed off the ball by slowing down the head of the racket on the follow through.
6   Watch the ball carefully and maintain balance throughout the stroke.

Problems and solutions

Dropshot problems occur because players either try to hit the ball with too much force or try to use a 'flicky' wrist action which results in a loss of racket head control. Practise your dropshots and try to develop this 'feel' of the ball on the racket.

Practice

Set up a routine with your partner, both playing dropshots in the service boxes.
Bring in more angle on the dropshot rather as for the drive routines but with the use of the dropshot instead. Use target areas to improve your control and accuracy.

THE SLICE SERVICE

Very often when players first make the change to a chopper grip they find that they automatically slice the ball, sometimes with too much slice, as the flexibility in the wrist has to be developed. However, once this has been mastered, it is well worthwhile developing the use of slice on both serves but *mainly* on your second service. This can force your opponent either to return a ball which is swerving into his body or one that stretches him wide to recover. Either way it can affect his normal routine and take him out of the normal hitting position. The lower bounce of the ball may also often cause problems.

John McEnroe prepares for a slice service

1 Stand in your *normal* service *position* using the *chopper* grip.
2 Place the ball in the air *slightly* more to the *right* of you than for a first service and *slightly* in *front* of you.
3 Bring your racket back to a *normal throwing position* and then by keeping the racket face in a semi-closed position bring the strings vigorously *round the outside of the ball*.
4 Listen to the *sound* your racket makes against the ball. You should be able to hear the distinctive noise of heavy spin!
5 Follow through with your racket in the normal way, allowing your body weight to transfer forward.

85

Problems and solutions

1 If you keep your racket face too closed on impact, you will find the ball will go too low and will travel too far towards the left. It may be necessary in the early stages to aim further to the right than normal to counteract the initial loss of direction. *Throw* vigorously round the *outside of the ball* so that the ball has the momentum to travel firmly towards the service box.
2 Conversely, if you find you are not imparting enough slice, try to develop a better wrist action so that the racket head travels through the air at a greater speed.

Practice

Use the target practices outlined and as with the topspin second service play points first using only one service and then use a first serve followed by your slice second serve. This should help your confidence to use this service during a match.

THE SLICE LOB

In extreme defence it is useful to be able to impart slice on your lobs. This will tend to keep the ball in the air longer, giving you more time to recover your court position. Also the spin may cause problems for the net player.

Jimmy Connors at full stretch

THE SLICE FOREHAND LOB

1　Use your basic forehand grip, though again western grip players may consider adjusting to either the eastern forehand grip or the continental grip.
2　Prepare early, keeping the *racket head* well *above* the hitting height of the ball.
3　*Open* the racket face and swing *downwards through and under* the ball.

4　Try to contact the ball as early as possible although under extreme pressure this may not be easy.
5　Keep the wrist *firm* and the racket face *open*.
6　Try to have the feeling of *holding the ball* on the strings for as long as possible. Follow through *upwards*.

THE SLICE BACKHAND LOB

1　Use a similar *grip* to the *basic drive*.
2　Prepare early, keeping the racket head well *above* the hitting height of the ball.
3　*Open* the racket face and swing *downwards* through and under the ball.
4　Try to contact the ball as *early* as possible.

5　Keep the *wrist firm* and the *racket face open*.
6　Try to have the feeling of holding the ball on the strings for as long as possible. Use a long follow through *upwards*.

THE SLICE TWO HANDED BACKHAND LOB

Only in extreme circumstances will a two handed player use slice on a lob as usually topspin will be preferable. However, should the emergency arise, consider the following points.

1 Use similar *grips* as for *basic* backhand.
2 Prepare as early as possible, keeping the racket head *above the ball* and the racket face *open*.
3 Hit *downwards, through and under* the ball.
4 Try to imagine keeping contact with the ball for as long as possible.
5 Keep the *wrist firm* and the racket face *open*.
6 Follow through high.

Problems and solutions

Lack of racket head control is often a major factor when lobbing unsuccessfully with slice. Often you are slicing a ball when under pressure and in this situation it is often possible to lose your balance and allow the wrist to go loose. Allow your weight to go forwards into the shot. Keep a firm wrist and take your racket back high and as early as possible in order to play a soundly prepared shot.

Lack of direction is often due to a rushed follow through. Make the follow through long and high.

Practice

Use the drills outlined for the lob but progress to a more pressurized practice against a net player when you are forced to move quickly and consequently have less time to play the lob. Try to create the same pressure situation repeatedly in order to develop your understanding of the racket work needed to play this lob successfully.

THE SLICE SMASH

This can be a particularly effective shot, as it gives you the opportunity to play a more *subtle, angled* smash, rather than the more powerful basic smash. The use of spin will also help you to control the ball.

1 Use your basic *chopper* grip.
2 Prepare early.
3 Move well to keep the ball to the *right* of your body.
4 *Close* the racket face slightly and bring the strings round the *side* of the ball similar to the sliced service.

5 Keep the ball in front of you so that your body weight can transfer into the shot.
6 Follow through with the racket travelling over to the left side of the body.

Problems and solutions

If you position yourself incorrectly underneath the ball you will have problems with your smash. Move quickly and well to put the ball on the *right* and slightly in *front* of you.

A late contact point is often due to poor movement and late racket preparation. *Prepare early*.

Lack of spin on the ball may be caused by insufficient brushing action round the side of the ball. Again listen for the *sound* of the spin.

Practice

With a partner, practise angled lobs and smashes. Give yourself a short target area in front of the service line and then a deeper target area in the corner near baseline and sideline. The sliced smash can be particularly useful in doubles, so practise your smash into the tramlines as well.

Having looked in detail at imparting spin on all the basic shots, it is still worth remembering that players will develop their own preference for the use of a certain type of spin on certain shots. Whilst the complete tennis player needs to be as versatile in his stroke technique as possible, it is important to remember that in a match situation you should use the shots that you know to be effective. Remember that to be able to use any spin effectively, a great deal of time must be spent on the practice court with a partner who will give you the opportunity to practise, improve or consolidate your shots.

Sometimes too much choice can lead to poor decision making. If you are able to play slice and topspin competently you must still try to react instinctively rather than always pre-planning your shots. Spin will add variety to your strokeplay but it must still be consistent and effective.

Court surfaces will also affect your decision making on the type of spin to use. Low bouncing, damp courts, particularly grass courts, make the use of slice most effective, whereas the higher bouncing synthetic surfaces lend themselves to the use of topspin.

Finally, remember that matches are won on the competitive court whatever the surface, but the groundwork is done on the practice court.

Part Three: Stroke variations

Now that we have mastered the basic fundamentals of technique and tactics let us take a look at the stroke variations which may be used in certain areas of the court in matchplay.

Sound shot selection is essential if you are to be a competent matchplayer. Therefore high level players should practise not only the basic shots and variations but also the alternative, sometimes 'rescue' shots which are a part of a successful player's game. These shots could be termed 'hybrids' of the basic technique and are really only successful if the player has already achieved a sound method of hitting.

Assuming that you are playing on a fairly fast tennis surface and you have a reasonably competent all-court game your main strategy should be to try to reach the net. This may involve an immediate move to the net, having served, or alternatively you may have to play a sound approach shot from the mid-court area before you are able to reach this attacking net position. Your opponent may well have the same tactic in mind, so within a rally both players may be forced to move back as well as forward and may have to set up attacking passing shots from the back of the court. Let us look at the stroke variations needed in the different areas of the court.

Base line

SERVICE AND MOVEMENT TO THE NET

If you are planning to run in to the net, having served, consider the following points:

1 Decide where you are aiming in your opponent's service box. A wide angled service should force the receiver to move

out of the court, thus leaving a wider space in which to play your first volley.

2 Your ball placement should be slightly further forward so that your attacking move can begin as soon as you strike the ball.

3 Take a long stride into the court with your right foot and move forward quickly.

4 Observe the receiver closely and when he is about to make contact with the ball, check your move forward with a 'split step' and then move forward again as you play your volley.

5 Try to reach the service line by the time the opponent makes his return. The slower your run forward the more chance you will have to play a difficult low ball on your next shot.

6 If your service is a second service you may be able to advance much further up the court before you play your next shot.

7 Move in to the net following the line of your service. Never forget that you are moving forward to play another shot so keep your racket in a ready position in preparation for your first volley or next shot.

8 Remember that a wide angled serve takes your opponent out of court but can also set up the chance of an angled return. Angles create angles!

9 A service down the centre line may well produce a straighter return to the incoming volleyer, but only if the service has landed with good length in the service box. A poor length service will allow the receiver far more choice of return and will consequently put the incoming volleyer under great pressure.

Becker places the ball well forward

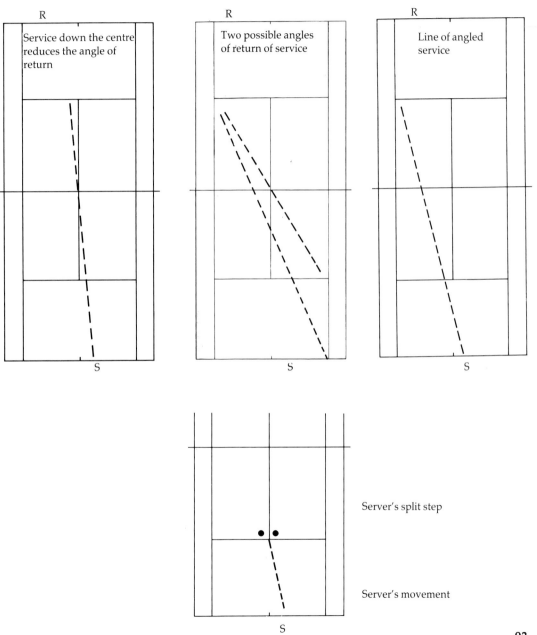

R

Service down the centre reduces the angle of return

R

Two possible angles of return of service

R

Line of angled service

S

S

S

Server's split step

Server's movement

S

Becker moves forward to the net having served

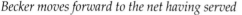

10 Players have favourite returns of service so it is worthwhile studying your potential opponents so that you have an understanding of their probable shot selection.

Problems and solutions

Thinking about following your service in to the net may make you lose the rhythm of your service and promptly serve a fault. Concentrate on being well balanced and rhythmical as you hit your service, and then move in. If you move too much before you strike the ball this will often result in an over hit service.

A low ball placement may mean that you hit too much over the ball and thus fail to get it over the net. Concentrate on good ball placement *slightly* in front of you.

Practice

Practise your first service with the move forward to at least a mid-court position. Then progress to playing the first volley after serving. Concentrate on target areas within the box.

If your service is not forceful enough for you to follow it to the net you may have to play the rally from the back of the court and take the initiative with an attacking shot played from a back-court position. Alternatively it may be impossible to attack at all. If you are well behind your base line and under pressure, a 'rescue' shot may be the only solution. In these crisis situations you may have to forget orthodox technique and alter your body position, balance, footwork and even racket grip.

THE LOW PASS

Your opponent may have been able to play an attacking return of service and thus take control of the net position. You then have certain options:

The low passing shot can be particularly effective if played early and with confidence. It is often played as a straight shot down the sideline as a reply to a wide angled volley.

1 Racket preparation must be quick and early.

2 Move swiftly to the ball, concentrating on a hitting area well in front of the body.

3 Swing through positively, keeping your body well balanced throughout the shot.

McEnroe is beaten by a low passing shot

Becker prepares to play a backhand passing shot. Notice the shoulder turn

Noah plays a forehand volley at the ideal hitting height – to be avoided when playing a passing shot

4 Keep your eyes on the ball throughout the stroke. *Never* lift your head as you are hitting to see your target area. This so often leads to failure on what must be a hard aggressive shot if it is to beat the volleyer.

5 Play the ball as near the net band as you dare, preferably using topspin, which will ensure that even if your opponent reaches your passing shot it will be a difficult low ball.

Problems and solutions

A high shot over the net will give your opponent the opportunity to play an easier volley at any angle he chooses.

Late racket preparation, slow movement to the ball and a lack of courage really to hit out are all reasons for failure on this shot.

Practice

Start with simple passing shots. Aim into the corner of the service box to practise dipping the ball. As you improve, get a partner, or even a ball machine, to feed *wide* angled shots. Move from the centre of the court at speed and go for this attacking shot down the line on the run.

Practise your forehand passing shot first. Progress to backhand and then play alternate forehand and backhand.

Finally try to respond to a simple but random feed set up by your partner so that the low pass is still possible.

Becker strides out to play a forehand passing shot

Recovery shots

If you are unable to play an attacking shot from the back of the court you may in an emergency be forced to play some form of recovery shot to keep you in the rally.

Under pressure there is little time to think of the perfect hitting area. Survival is the most important thing!

DEFENSIVE GROUNDSTROKES

Pam Shriver with her weight back plays a defensive backhand

These shots played under pressure may need to be hit with a slightly adjusted technique. Sometimes they may require a late hitting area with body weight usually on the back foot.

Problems and solutions

Because of the lack of time the backswing may be incomplete, causing the player to hit down on the ball into the net.

Because of the changed pattern of swing and follow through, the racket face may be too open, with the result that the ball goes out of court.

As the body weight is moving 'off' the shot rather than into it there is a tendency to lift your head and thus lose control of the shot. Concentrate on keeping a firm grip so that racket face control can still be maintained.

Practice

Stand in the 'no man's land' area of the court between service line and base line and get a partner to feed fairly hard deep balls from the net which you must attempt to play from a difficult position and in a hurry.

GROUNDSTROKE RECOVERY FROM THE LOB

If your opponent has played a high lob it is sometimes possible to move back very quickly, overtaking the ball, and rather than lobbing back play a *surprise* hard ground stroke.

This shot will possibly have a very late impact, and as you are moving back quickly your body weight may be falling away from the target area.

Concentrate on maintaining balance as well as you can and keep a firm grip on the racket to ensure a *controlled racket face*.

Problems and solutions

The main problem is that you are under pressure and must keep control of the ball

despite your poor body position and lack of balance.

Make every effort to get your weight into the shot and swing through *positively*.

Concentrate on the points mentioned above, be brave in your outlook and this positive reply will probably succeed.

Practice

Start from the net, get your partner to lob the ball over your head, move back quickly and play this aggressive groundstroke. Remember this is a tactic to use as a surprise counter attack! Do not overplay this shot, although sometimes attack is the best form of defence.

FOREHAND OPEN STANCE

Boris Becker plays a forehand from an open stance position

Ivan Lendl plays an open stance forehand but still maintains balance

Sometimes if you are pulled out of the court to retrieve a very wide angled ball it is necessary to have the racket to meet the ball as quickly as possible and this is easier if the body stance remains 'open', that is, facing the net. The contact point will be nearer to the body and usually parallel with the body. The racket should swing from the right of the body to the left, i.e. 'out' to 'in', as the body weight transfers from the right foot to the left foot.

Problems and solutions

As the racket is swinging across the body it is often more difficult to maintain balance and also control the racket. Keep your grip firm and imagine you are leaning in on the shot.

A common problem with this shot is the tendency to play it with too much spin, i.e. sidespin or topspin.

If you don't put enough weight into it, the shot may lack penetration and length.

Practice

Try using an open stance forehand in a fairly easy situation on the court. As your control improves progress to practise under more pressure.

Start from the centre of the back line and get a partner to drive a ball to a wide angle across court which you must then move to quickly and return across the court.

Then practise the same set up, hitting down the line.

The mid court

If you have managed to force your opponent to play a return into the middle of the court now is the time to capitalize on this weak reply and make your forward attack to the net.

THE GROUNDSTROKE APPROACH SHOT

McEnroe plays a backhand approach shot and moves forward to the net

Stroke variations

Notice the hitting area well forward when McEnroe shapes up to play a backhand approach shot

Becker pivots sideways as he prepares to play a backhand approach shot

Whether you are playing a forehand or backhand drive, it is likely that you will choose to hit this shot with spin to give you extra control of the ball. You may often decide to use a slice approach shot, as when the bounce of the ball is low you will find it easier to play and control your approach shot by using slice. However, if you are confident in your use of topspin and the bounce of the ball is sufficiently high, then attack with a topspin approach shot. A successful player will be able to play either topspin or slice, as the situation requires.

The *hitting area* for a successful approach shot should be slightly further in front of you than for the normal drive.

Good footwork is important in order to get in the correct hitting area and it is essential to remain well balanced as your body weight 'leans in' on the shot.

If the ball is low bend your knees and keep your head down as you strike the ball in order to *maintain your balance*.

When using slice aim to play the ball nearer to the top of the net to keep it low, and direct it deep to one of the corners of the court, preferably your opponent's weaker side.

When using topspin, you should hit the ball higher over the net, as the topspin will force it down into the court. You may even try a short angled approach shot.

Remember that because you are closer to the net you have a shorter amount of court to hit into, so beware of overhitting.

Approach shots must be played with great precision. Having struck the ball move forward quickly to a ready position at the net, watching your opponent carefully to see what he plans to do. A good approach shot should force an easy return which you can put away with a winner.

Problems and solutions

It is very easy to rush and snatch at the shot in your anxiety to move to the net quickly. Take your time. Find a good hitting position and try to play a well balanced, controlled shot.

Practice

Have your partner play a ball near to your service line so that you can move in to play an approach shot. Practise approach shots to both corners of the court, using both straight and cross court approach shots. Try a linking exercise where you play a drive from the base line, an approach shot from the mid court and then move forward to play a volley.

THE HALF VOLLEY

Sometimes in the mid-court area, a player will find that he is not quite close enough to the ball to play a volley and so he is forced to play a shot just off the ground, namely a half volley. The hitting area for the half volley should be as far forward as possible and the ball should be struck very low, just as it bounces up from the ground.

Move quickly so that you can get in as good a hitting position as possible and try to keep your head down and your body balanced. The racket should be kept steady as with a normal volley but to keep

Noah plays a backhand half volley

control of the ball allow some forward swing. Try to play the half volley as a safe controlled approach shot and keep it as deep in your opponent's court as possible. Follow the shot to the net.

Problems and solutions

This shot requires a quick reflex action to get the racket to the ball as quickly as possible. Poor positioning can result in a lack of control. A 'flicky' emergency use of the wrist will also tend to make the ball lose depth and direction. Keep your wrist firm so that you can control the racket face.

Avoid 'opening' or closing the racket face too much.

Practice

Stand just inside the service box and with a partner at the base line hitting low hard drives to you, try to take the ball early on the half volley whenever possible. Move forward quickly to the ball so that you strike it just as it comes off the bounce. This is an extremely difficult practice to set up: it may be necessary for your partner to throw the ball by hand to ensure accuracy.

THE DRIVE VOLLEY

This is a shot similar to a drive, but played on the volley, when you have a lot of time and are about to move into the attack. It is particularly useful as a counter attack to a high floating return from your opponent. Rather than standing back and waiting for the ball to bounce, move forward quickly and strike the ball as a drive volley.

Prepare early as you would for a drive, but with slightly less backswing.

Strike the ball well forward, allowing your body weight to go into the shot and move on forward to the net having played your drive volley.

Swing the racket through positively. Drive volleys will often be hit with slight topspin to aid control of the ball.

Follow through as you move toward the net.

Pay particular attention to your target area

in your opponent's court. Aim to play the shot with power away from your opponent. Follow through in the direction of the shot. Sometimes a shorter angled drive volley can catch your opponent by surprise and prove to be an outright winner.

Problems and solutions

It is essential to choose the right time to play this shot! Wait for a high floating ball. If you rush and pick a ball which is dropping low you will find it extremely difficult to hit the drive volley over the net and into the court.

Remember only high *slow* balls should be considered when there is time to take the racket well back. The harder ball must still be hit with the shorter punch volley.

As with all shots, beware of losing balance as you strike the ball. Keep good control of the racket face by maintaining a firm grip.

The drive volley is more often played on the forehand side but a two handed backhand drive volley can be especially effective.

Because it has a longer swing than normal volleys the drive volley can easily be mistimed.

The drive volley is often hit too late.

Practice

Get your partner to give you a very easy high floating drive and move in quickly and play a drive volley.

Use a sequence where you rally from the back of the court and then select the correct ball on which to attack.

THE BACKHAND SMASH

If there is time it is always advisable to try to move quickly around the ball so that the stronger forehand smash can be played. However, on occasions there will be no time and therefore it is essential that you play the ball with a backhand smash.

Use the normal backhand grip and side step back quickly underneath the ball.

Make a strong shoulder turn and bring the racket forward to meet the ball squarely and in front of the body.

Reach high and allow a sharp wrist action to bring the racket head over the ball.

Problems and solutions

This shot requires quick movement and a very firm shoulder and wrist action. Poor movement will result in a late hitting area

which can lead to lack of racket head control. Concentrate on moving well and keeping the ball well in front of you.

Practice

Stand in the mid-court area and get your partner to lob toward the left hand back corner of the court. Move in and play your backhand smash.

As your control improves progress to a sequence of volley and backhand smash.

Finally use a random practice where your partner can lob over your left shoulder whenever he choses.

This shot will help you to retain an attacking position but you must practise it to gain confidence.

THE JUMP SMASH

This smash can be used effectively to keep a forward position at the net.

Use the basic technique required for the normal smash but in order to keep the ball in front of you when you strike it remember you need to spring up quickly so good balance is essential.

Remember to *side-step* back underneath the ball so you can then jump up from a balanced 'launching pad'.

Problems and solutions

This smash must be hit quickly when the ball is above you. Quick movement backwards is therefore essential. Poor move-

Martina Navratilova reaches for a jump smash

ment is often the chief cause for failure. Avoid jumping up with your body still square to the net. This will cause loss of balance and control.

Practice

Stand close to the net and get your partner to lob a high slow ball over your head. Reach up for the jump smash and then move forwards again quickly.

Progress to practising a routine in which you play a low volley and then have to reach up quickly to play a jump smash.

Finally progress to a random volley smash practice where again you have to move back quickly in order to retrieve the lob.

THE DROPSHOT

As has already been mentioned a dropshot is played with underspin to just clear the net and land near the net in the opponent's half of the court. It requires a gentle but firm touch. Occasionally your opponent may play a dropshot which will bring you forward to the net and a counter dropshot can be an effective reply, particularly if he is still at the back of the court.

As with all dropshots control of the racket face is extremely important.

Use the basic grips as for drives and prepare for the stroke as if you were going to play a drive. Stroke the face of the racket down the back and underneath the ball. Take the speed off the ball so that it just drops over the net.

Problems and solutions

As the ball from your opponent is likely to have backspin on it remember to get down to the ball by bending your knees. Early racket preparation is essential. If you are late on the shot it is likely to go into the net.

Practice

Get your partner to play a short shot near the net and play a counter dropshot. In order to practise these strokes which can be played from the three main areas of the court, try to set up some drills which will give you the opportunity to link all three areas together.

Start from the shots at the back of the court and then try to move forward using the mid-court and net shots as they occur. One of the most essential aspects of successful matchplay is to be quick and versatile in decision making, namely making the correct shot selection in the shortest possible time. Only with thorough and regular practice can you gain the necessary confidence in your strokemaking. Then the correct and effective selection of your best shots will become a natural part of your game plan.

Noah opens the racket face and plays a backhand dropshot

At the net

Having looked at the shots played from the back-and mid-court areas let us move on to a range of shots which you may need to use when you move closer to the net.

Apart from the basic volley and smash which we have already studied the following stroke variations should come into play when you are at the net.

THE LOW VOLLEY

You have no doubt discovered that the easiest volley to play is when the ball is struck at approximately shoulder height. Knowing this your opponent is more likely to try to keep the ball very low over the net and it is then that you must reach down to play a successful low volley.

From the ready position move forward quickly to meet the ball well in front of you. An early and balanced hitting area is vital to the success of this shot.

Bend your knees to get down to this low ball.

Open the racket face so that your volley can still clear the net.

You will be hitting from below the height of the net but it is essential to keep the wrist firm so that the racket face controls the ball. For extra control, use a little backspin.

Remember if you are playing a crosscourt angle then the ball must be struck well forward.

Tactically there are a number of different target areas which you should consider, depending on your opponent's position.

Martina Navratilova bends to play a low forehand volley

McEnroe lunges forward for a low forehand volley

A low volley should generally be played deep to the back corners to keep the opponent under pressure.

Alternatively a shorter angled volley can be particularly effective.

Problems and solutions

As always quick movement is essential. A failure to get down to the low ball will often result in a volley into the net. Bend quickly.

Practice

Set up a volley rally with your partner trying to keep the ball as low over the net as possible. Set up a drive to volley rally, with your partner driving to keep the ball as low over the net as possible.

Edburg bends low for a backhand volley.

Connors plays a low backhand volley

THE STOP VOLLEY

Navratilova shapes up to play a forehand stop volley

McEnroe well balanced for a backhand stop volley

This shot can be particularly effective as it can take the opponent by surprise and leave him stranded on his heels. Keep to the technique of the basic volley whether a forehand or backhand but keep the wrist very firm and open the racket face at impact to increase backspin.

Reduce the follow through so that the ball just drops over the net.

This shot should be played off a ball which is net high or below and requires a good control of the racket face, sometimes called good 'touch'.

Problems and solutions

It is essential that the ball drops very short in the opponent's court. If you play it too deep you are likely to be passed at the net! It is essentially a surprise shot and should never be overused. A loose wrist can result in a high loose volley. Remember to keep the wrist firm and keep a very short movement with the racket.

Practice

With a partner stand about 6 feet (2 metres) apart and gently tap the ball to each other. Progress to your partner moving back to drive the ball fairly hard to you but still try to play a stop volley into a target area some 3 to 4 feet (1 metre) from the net. Progress to setting up a drive and volley routine and select the right ball on which to play a stop volley. Put down a target some 3–4 feet (1 metre) from the net and see if your stop volley can land in this area.

THE LOB VOLLEY

Jordan opens the racket face for a backhand lob volley

This is a shot which should be used when both you and the opponent are close to the net in a volleying exchange. As a means of surprise rather than trying to outvolley the net player use a lob volley which, if played sufficiently high, should be a winning shot. However, remember it must be played high enough to travel over the opponent's head and into the court. If he is able to smash it then he may be able to play the certain winner! Use the technique as for the basic volley but keeping your wrist firm open the racket face at impact to give the ball height over the opponent's head.

Keep your knees bent and maintain balance throughout the stroke. To keep control of the ball allow a short follow through. This again is a shot which requires a fine 'touch'.

Not a shot to be used too often or on a day when your 'touch' is unreliable!

Problems and solutions

If you fail to give the ball sufficient height over the net then you will set up a very easy lob for your opponent to smash. Remember to open the racket face but keep your wrist firm.

Practice

Set up a volley routine at the net. Play three volleys and then on the fourth play a lob volley and see if your partner can play it back into court. Then repeat.

Connors lunges forward for a backhand lob volley. Notice the almost horizontal racket face

111

JANE POYNDER AND CHARLES APPLEWHAITE

Part Four: Matchplay strategy

Once you have mastered the basic techniques of shot making and understand the simple tactics required in both singles and doubles play, you should now try to improve your understanding of the matchplay of tennis.

But first it is important that you make an honest analysis of your own game. This should include not only an evaluation of your performance on court, but an understanding of your physical and mental capabilities.

As a quality player you should be capable of playing your own favourite game with regularity. This should be based on sound principles and should become your normal method of play. However, you must be able to adapt this method to suit the varying conditions and opponents you may encounter.

It is also essential to look at how the different types of court surface affect the type of game you play. Finally, try to get some advance information on your opponent's game and his strengths and weaknesses.

Self analysis

STRENGTHS

First consider all the good points in your game. To be a successful player you must have confidence in your own ability to succeed. Use a positive approach in your analysis. A negative outlook will only help to destroy your self confidence. Self doubt is the most difficult opponent to overcome!

TYPE OF GAME
Consider where you like to be on the court. Are you a base line player or do you prefer to attack and move forward to the net?

STROKES

Which strokes do you have the most confidence in? A well grooved stroke should be working for you as well in the final set as in the knock up.

PHYSICAL FITNESS

Are you physically fit and well prepared for the match?

WINNING SHOTS

Given the right opportunity where do you like to play your outright winning shots?

COURT CONDITIONS

What is your favourite surface and how well are you able to adapt to either slower or faster court conditions?

OPPONENTS

Which type of opponent do you like to play against? Do you cope well with the player who rushes the net or do you prefer to play against a base line player?

Chris Lloyd – an extremely successful baseline player

MENTAL APPROACH

Are you relaxed and mentally well prepared?

McEnroe plays a well grooved forehand drive

WEAKNESSES

Having looked at the good points in your game, consider honestly the areas which tend to let you down. Analyse why you have these weaknesses. It may not be just a problem in your stroke technique, especially if flaws appear in your game only under certain conditions in a match. This may be due to physical fatigue or loss of concentration due to anxiety. It may be that your opponent's tactical analysis of your game has been more effective than yours of his!

All these areas of weakness can be improved if you face up to them honestly. The player who loses matches but who always finds a reason for the loss outside himself will seldom improve.

Finally you should accept that there will be occasions when you meet an opponent who is undoubtedly a better tennis player than you. If you accept that you may lose but try to learn something from this loss which will help you in the future then even a defeat can turn into a minor victory!

THE OPPONENT

Having analysed your own game it is worthwhile studying that of your opponent. If you are encountering him for the first time an early check list can be helpful.

The right handed Becker takes up a serving position

Lendl looking strong and fit

Consider the following points in the practice time before you begin the match.

1 Physique. Does he look strong and fit?

2 Is he right or left handed? Does he use a two handed backhand?

3 Does he move well to the ball?

4 Are his groundstrokes consistent from the base line?

5 Does he seem keen to come to the net?

6 Does he volley and smash with confidence?

7 Does he have a smooth, rhythmical service action?

8 Does he use both slice and topspin in his game?

9 Are there any apparent flaws in his stroke technique even in the practice?

10 Does he appear relaxed and confident?

The left handed McEnroe is beaten by a passing shot

Mandlikova plays a slice backhand

Boris Becker plays a topspin forehand

COURT CONDITIONS

Although the playing conditions are obviously the same for both players, some court conditions will suit one player more than the other.

FAST COURT SURFACES

Grass
Wood
Some forms of indoor carpet courts
Non porous cement
A fast court surface tends to keep the bounce of the ball low. The ball will also tend to bounce off the surface more quickly and this means that the player has less time to play his shots. Net players will favour a fast court.

MEDIUM FAST SURFACES

Most indoor surfaces which are often made of a rubberised carpet or carpet itself.
The bitumen based all-weather courts which are sprayed with a rubberised paint.
The outdoor synthetic 'grass' types of court.
On a medium fast court the bounce of the ball still tends to be reasonably low and will come off the ground fairly quickly, but all these surfaces will respond to the use of spin and make an advance to the net possible.

SLOW SURFACES

The loose type of top dressing used on some tarmac courts and also on shale and clay.
Porous cement all-weather courts which have no top dressing.
The bounce on these courts tends to be slower and higher. This gives a player more time to get to the ball and play his shots but also makes the more attacking net game less effective. On a slow surface the rallies will tend to be longer and a player must exercise patience in order to keep the ball in play.
It is likely that you will have to play matches on a variety of court surfaces and while you may have a particular preference it is important to understand (a) the type of bounce you will encounter and (b) the type of game you must employ in these varying conditions.
If you are reluctant to adapt to changing court conditions you will be at a disadvantage.

WEATHER CONDITIONS

While far more tennis is played now in indoor centres where only the temperature and lighting may cause problems, many tennis matches are held outside in less than favourable weather conditions. Rain and snow may cause play to cease but excessive wind must be coped with as unless the court surface is unfit then the weather will still be regarded as 'officially fine' no matter what the force of the gale! Therefore, it is essential that you learn to use the wind to your advantage.

WIND
Always check to see which way the wind is blowing. A wind gusting straight up and down the court may make an advance to the net impossible at one end and imperative at the other. The use of spin will help you to control the ball in windy conditions. The sidewind blowing across the court can be used most effectively on angled shots.

SUN
The angle of the sun may prove to be difficult and may make serving and smashing more of a problem than usual when sighting the ball. Again remember this when you are lobbing your opponent. A high lob which forces him to look straight up to the sun may give you a well earned point.

RAIN
While torrential rain may stop play, matches may be resumed as soon as the rain stops and this may mean that you have to move on a slippery surface. Obviously on a grass court this will mean that the bounce of the ball will be even lower and even on a hard surface the balls will tend to pick up the moisture from the court and will bounce lower and feel 'heavier' on the racket. In this situation, even your most powerfully hit drives may feel an effort and may drop well short of your expected target area.

Finally remember that conditions and court surfaces can change within a match. Try to be adaptable in your match strategy in order to be able to cope with variable conditions whatever they may be.

Virginia Wade feels the cold

John McEnroe feels the heat

Singles match strategy

Always try to start a match with some form of *match plan* in mind. This may have to be adjusted as the match develops but some of the following strategies may help you along the road to winning.

Singles court positions

COURT POSITIONS

Try to start a rally from the best possible vantage point and within the rally try to maintain as good a court position as you are able. The singles base line measures

Matchplay strategy

27 feet (8½ metres) and to cover this well it is important to try to recover to a central position after each shot.

SERVING

Serve from a position approximately a foot (30cm) from the centre of the base line and unless you move immediately to the net, recover to approximately 3 to 4 feet (1 metre) behind the base line as the rally develops.

Navratilova prepares to serve from the right side

McEnroe moves to the net having served

Mandlikova prepares to serve from the left side

120

RECEIVING

Receive the service from just behind the base line; but if you know your opponent has a particularly hard service stand even further back so that when you strike the ball you are still able to move forward to play your return. Avoid putting yourself in a position where you are forced to return the service with your weight moving backwards and off balance. Take up a receiving position half way between the centre of the base line and the sideline. Try not to show that you have a preference for receiving the service on your forehand wing as this may advertise the fact that you have a weaker backhand.

Again, like the server, try to recover to a central court position just behind the base line as the rally develops.

NO MAN'S LAND

The area between the service line and base line is often referred to as 'no man's land'. Although you will have to play many shots from this area of the court it is important that you are not caught standing in this mid court area. Use it only as a temporary position that you have been *forced* into and having played the ball from the mid court area either return quickly to just behind the base line, or follow your approach shot in to the net. *Never get caught standing in 'no man's land'.*

PLAYING TO A WEAKNESS

If you have managed to find a weakness in your opponent's stroke technique or playing ability you should make every effort to expose this weakness. Be subtle in your approach! If you only play to his weakness

The receiver

you may find that his stroke will actually start to work better. Try to draw the opponent out of position and then play to his weaker side. This will give him less opportunity to run round and hide the weaker shot and by varying your hitting should help to keep the opponent in a state of anxiety and confusion.

MAKE THE OPPONENT RUN

Try to make sure that your opponent has little time in which to play his shots and, more importantly, that he has regularly to change position to play the same shots. It is easy to groove a stroke if you are always hitting from much the same area of the court but if you want to break up an opponent's rhythm it is necessary to move him around the court in all directions and preferably in a pattern he cannot anticipate. This should result in a lower success rate in his stroke making.

WRONG FOOTING YOUR OPPONENT

This can be one of the most satisfying aspects of tactical play. It follows directly from making your opponent run from side to side. First you need to make your opponent think that you are going to play to a regular pattern, then as he moves to anticipate your shot play your drive in the opposite direction, thus wrong footing him. However, observe your opponent's speed carefully. Only the quick footed will move early to anticipate an expected return. The slow opponent may not have moved at all and by returning the ball to the same part of the court you may be playing it straight back to him. Never a good tactic!

Connors playing a two handed backhand return of service

Noah plays a forehand return close to the body

NEVER CHANGE A WINNING GAME

This sounds a very obvious statement but many players do change a winning game and consequently lose the match. It is vital that if you are winning a match with a particular tactic then you should continue with this strategy. However, it requires great concentration to keep up the same plan throughout a match. Some players, getting over-confident, may try to experiment with 'clever' shots which in fact allow the opponent to win some unexpected points. This can ultimately put pressure on the player who was winning and can result in a complete turn around in the score.

Remember to keep your experimentation to your practice sessions and in matches win as quickly and effectively as you can.

Conversely it is poor tactics to keep on with a match plan which is obviously unsuccessful. If you are losing heavily to an opponent who appears to have the measure of your game and is not being inconvenienced at all by your method of play, it is essential that you evaluate what alternative action might help you to overcome this losing streak. Of course, your new tactic must be safely within your technical capabilities. It is no good deciding that the way to upset your opponent would be to rush to the net at every opportunity if you are quite unable to volley at the net when you get there. However, a sensible change of plan may well produce the desired result and a reversal in the match score. Be prepared to be flexible in your tactical thinking and discard a plan if it really is not working well for you.

UPSETTING YOUR OPPONENT'S RHYTHM

If you are winning a match with ease, you feel in total control of the situation and confident to play bold attacking shots, because you feel almost certain that they will succeed. On other occasions, when you are not in such an advantageous position in the match, you may find it almost impossible to develop any rhythm in your game. The racket feels as if it belongs to someone else and the ball never seems to be in quite the right hitting area. Players often think that this failure to perform well is solely their own fault – not realising that an experienced opponent can upset your rhythm so that you begin to suffer from uncertainty, indecision and, ultimately, poor performance. Try to upset your opponent in this way and thus sow the seeds of his destruction!

Keep your opponent guessing as to what you are going to do next.

Vary the *length of your shot*,
the *speed of your shot*,
the *spins you employ* and finally
the *pattern of your play*.

View your task as that of a *code breaker*. The code breaker is always looking for the constant key to the opponent's code. Meanwhile the opponent is often changing the rules of the code, thereby making the breaker's task much more difficult.

Winning tennis players put pressure on their opponents and never allow them time to evaluate their performance. *Keep your opponent guessing.*

NULLIFY YOUR OPPONENT'S STRENGTHS

Like you, your opponent has probably analysed his own game and will have certain 'favourite' shots on which he thinks he can rely. Often these are the winning shots and often he will try to play a rally so that he forces you to put the ball in his 'favourite' area from which the winning shot can be played. Make a special note of where your opponent plays these particularly good winning shots and try to make every possible effort to retrieve the ball by anticipating where the shot will be played. If you are able to return what he considered was an outright winner it will have in effect 'trumped' his 'ace' shot. This can undermine his confidence and may either force him to play an even harder shot which may produce an error, or make

Stefan Edburg attacks the net.

him try another shot in which he has less confidence. In either case you will have undermined his confidence and nullified this particular strength.

PRACTICES FOR IMPROVING MATCH TACTICS

Just as it is important to practise in order to improve your basic stroke technique, so is it essential to use practice routines which will help you in certain tactical situations. It is impossible to implement a new tactic successfully in a match if it has not already been honed and refined on the practice court.

ROLE PLAYING

If you are trying to introduce a new tactic into your game you must practise your new role both physically and mentally in order to add a new dimension to your game. If for instance you are a base line

player and find that you are losing matches on fast court surfaces because of your reluctance to come to the net, you must not only start practising a serve and volley routine but also try to think like an attacking, net rushing player.

The early stages of a rally can so often dictate who ultimately wins it that it is worth taking a close look at the shots that are needed in this situation. And as so much of modern tennis is played at the net it is essential to have a clear understanding of the tactics required for successful net play.

SERVE AND VOLLEY TACTICS

Connors attacks the net

An accomplished player must be able to use this strategy and should understand the principles related to it.

In a simple form, the server must put his service into play, move very quickly to the net and play a volley, hopefully, for a winner. First however, if this tactic is to succeed, you must have a positive approach.

1   Before taking your first service decide that you are going to serve and move forward to the net.

2   Make every effort to get your *first service* into court even if this means reducing its speed. Your opponent should be further behind the base line when awaiting your first service, so there is less likelihood that he will make a counter attack towards the net and therefore it will be easier for you to play your first volley.

If your first service is reasonably well placed and hard it should force a rather weaker return from the receiver.

3   Having moved forward as quickly as you can towards the net, try to check your run just as the receiver is about to make contact on his return.

4   If the return of service travels low over the net then your first low volley is unlikely to be played as a winner. Go for a well placed deep volley which should force the opponent to play a weak reply.

5   If the return of service is high, move forward quickly and try to make the first volley the winning shot of the rally.

Remember that you should concentrate on the two essential aspects of this net rushing tactic:

A   Get your first service regularly into play.

B   Make certain that your first volley goes into play.

THE RETURN OF SERVICE

Even if you have a particularly good service you will never be successful in matches if you are unable to break your opponent's serve. Therefore, the return of service is as vital as the service.

When receiving the service consider the following points:

1 Try to judge the speed and spin of the oncoming serve.

2 Anticipate whether the server is aiming for a wide angled service or one down the centre of the service box.

Mandlikova plays a backhand return of service

3 Observe carefully to see whether the server is planning to move forward having served or whether he is staying back.

4 Prepare as quickly as you can. Often the speed of the serve will give you very little hitting time so your racket preparation must be instantaneous. Too often the return of service is purely a 'reflex action'.

Remember the successful return of service must do the following:

1 The return *must* go into court.

2 If the server has moved forward try to keep your return as low over the net as possible so that you force the server to volley either near his feet or from a low stretched position.

3 If you have a fairly easy return try to play a passing shot to beat the incoming volleyer.

4 If the server has failed to move forward the return of service should be played sufficiently strongly to keep the opponent behind the base line.

5 If the service was short then the receiver should capitalize on this. Counter attack by moving forward to the net, using the return of service as a deep, well placed approach shot.

Remember the tactical advantage is with the server and the more the receiver can take away this advantage the more he will be able to change the balance of power within the rally in his own favour. The two essential aspects of the return of serve should be:

1 The return of serve *must* go into court.

2 The return must be played as well as possible to take away the initiative from the server.

ATTACKING THE NET

Obviously the amount a player attacks the net is related to his ability to play successful volleys and smashes from the net. Therefore, it is essential to build up your confidence in your net play before making frequent moves forward! However, once this has been achieved, the reasonably accomplished player should make moves to the net as part of his overall strategy. As a general rule, it is easier to hit a winner from the net than it is from the baseline, as the volleyer has a greater range of angles and has to hit the ball a shorter distance. However, to make it easier for the volleyer it is important to move to the net from a position of strength, namely with the opponent under pressure at the back of the court and being kept under pressure through a good length approach shot. It is pointless moving forward to the net if you play a poor length approach shot as you will only be passed or at best be given rather a difficult ball to volley. Remember that the foundation of a successful approach to the net is set up from the back of the court, either through an attacking first service or from a deep well placed approach drive.

PLAYING TO THE SCORE

You may often hear it said that certain top players manage to play the 'important points' well. What does that mean? Obviously all points carry the same value but in any game there are certain critical stages. If you are able to cope with a crisis and overcome it then you will in all probability go on to win the match. There is often a very fine dividing line between the winner and the loser and it is mainly down to how well a player copes in a particularly difficult situation.

IMPORTANT POINTS

While it obviously helps if you are able to win every point this is rarely the case unless you are very much stronger than your opponent. In a closely contested match where the score is level there are some critical points which *you* must try to win rather than your opponent. This is when you should try to keep to a 'percentage' shot which has a high chance of going in the court, rather than a more risky spectacular shot which may not succeed. Let us look at these 'important' points.

THE FIRST POINT IN A GAME

Always try to win the first point! It sounds obvious but psychologically it will immediately put your opponent under pressure.

THE FOURTH POINT

If you are leading 30–15 it is again vital that you make it 40–15. This will ease the pressure on your service and should make it easier for you to win the first game point. Another vital point to win! Get into the habit of winning a game on the first game point you have. This will add to your confidence in the 'tighter' later stages of the match.

PLAYING THE PERCENTAGES

If you do find yourself in a trouble spot, for example being game point down, it is vital that you have a recovery plan so that you can go on to win the game. But how can you reliably plan to get out of trouble and back into the match? The answer is that by knowing your own ability well you should know your chance of success or failure on a particular shot in a certain situation and when it is essential that you win the point you will use the shot which you know to be effective.

Let us look at an obvious example. The player serving has a fast first service and the receiver is standing just outside the baseline. If the player is a 'serve and volley' player and he manages to put his first serve into play the odds are very much in favour of the server. If the receiver manages to return the ball into play but above waist height to the incoming volleyer, then the odds are still in favour of the server winning the point. If, however, the receiver manages to return the ball into play low at the feet of the incoming volleyer, then the odds in favour of winning the point have shifted slightly in favour of the receiver. The receiver, therefore, knows that if he is to win the point he has to keep the ball low over the net and play it at the feet of the incoming server.

The percentage rule for the server is to put the maximum number of first balls into play and the percentage rule for the receiver is to keep the ball low at the feet or wide of the incoming server. If either player succeeds in putting a high percentage of his particular strategy into play, he will effectively have a better chance of winning the match.

The successful match player knows the percentage chance of success and failure in almost any given situation and will, therefore, have a better chance of making the right decisions. You must weigh the percentage shot against the risk. It is always better to fight back with a percentage shot rather than finding you are a game down because you chose the wrong shot. Experienced players find that by reducing the amount of risk they are able to withstand difficult moments in a match. The inexperienced player will tend just to play the ball irrespective of the score and will often suffer unfortunate consequences.

Chris Lloyd returns on the backhand and lets go with the left hand

Doubles match strategy

Many of the strategies and tactics already referred to will apply whether you are playing singles or doubles. However, there are some important points to consider if you are to be a successful doubles player.

Remember that the game of doubles is essentially a *team effort*. Two individuals on the same side of the net will never make a successful doubles pair unless they can blend as a team and their style of play is compatible.

If you are always blaming your partner because you feel he has let you down then it is unlikely that your partnership will be a great success. It is also unusual for both players to play at their best at the same time! Therefore, you must take the rough with the smooth and help your partner when he is having a bad patch in the hope that he will help you when you are not at your best.

COURT POSITIONS

As in singles play, good court positions are vital. Ideally two players should be able to cover the width of the doubles court with ease. After all in singles one player is able to cover 27 feet (8½ metres) and in doubles you only have an extra 9 feet (2¾ metres) to cover with the help of a partner. You are really responsible for half of the court each, so at the start of a rally take up positions which are best suited to covering the whole court.

If you are serving you should stand halfway between the inner tram line and the centre service line. Your partner should stand in a volleying positon at the net about 3–4 feet (1 metre) from the inner side line. The receiving player should stand just outside the base line midway between the tram line and the centre service line while his partner should take up a position halfway between his tram line and the

centre service line, just inside the service line, not as close to the net as the server's partner.

PLAYING AS A TEAM
Control of the net is vital in doubles and both teams should have this in mind. If the service is good the server should move immediately to the net. The receiving pair will then take up a more defensive position at the back of the court. If the receiver is able to take the initiative and move to the net on the return of service then both he *and his partner* should move to the net and the serving team should move back.

Although you do not usually start off in a position on a level with your partner, as the rally develops you should try to be aware of your partner's court position and should try to move as he moves. Ideally

will mean that he is playing the ball on his forehand side. Of course, if the right court player's backhand is a stronger shot than the left court player's forehand, then the opposite would apply.

And when at the net it is usually the player nearer the ball and in the most attacking position who should go for the shot.

PLAYING WITH A LEFT HANDER

If you are right handed and have a left handed partner then you must decide on the most effective formation for you. Sometimes it is tactically beneficial to have the strength of two forehands down the middle area of the court. In this situation it works better if the left hander receives service from the right hand court. However, if you are worried about your ability to return the service effectively, it may be better if the left handed player takes the left court. It is sometimes more difficult to cope with a wide angled service on the backhand rather than the forehand side.

THE USE OF ANGLES

Doubles is very much a game of angles. If you are able to break up the team work of the opposition by playing a wide angled shot, it should give your partner the opportunity to volley into the empty space between the opponents. For this reason doubles is essentially a matter of team work, with one player trying to open up the court for his partner to play a winner into the space.

DOMINATION OF THE NET

The net position is vitally important in doubles strategy. Try to get nearer to the net than your opponents so that you can

you should feel as if you and your partner are joined together by a piece of string and if one player is moved in one direction then the partner should move in the same direction as well so that your court is well covered. This applies particularly if your partner is pulled out of position by a wide angled return. You must then move across to cover the potential shot down the centre of the court – always a problem area in doubles.

HOW TO COVER THE MIDDLE AREA

Assuming that both partners are right handed it is usual that the player taking the left court should take the balls travelling down the centre of the court as this

hit down while they are forced to hit the ball upwards. It is far easier to play winning shots if the ball is at shoulder height rather than at knee height.

KEEP THE BALL LOW OVER THE NET

Even when playing groundstrokes try to keep your returns as low over the net as possible. This again will force the opponents to hit the ball upwards and should give you the opportunity to put the ball away as a winner.

ATTACK THE WEAKER OPPONENT

It has already been mentioned that it is likely that one player will not be performing as well as his partner. Be aware of this and seize on every opportunity to exploit the weaker partner.

Pam Shriver putting the lob to good use

Mandlikova making every effort to return the service

position at the net. Make every effort to get your first service into play. This should force the receiving side into playing a defensive return which the server's partner might be able to intercept and hit a volley winner.

THE USE OF THE LOB
The lob can be an especially effective shot in doubles. It can break up even the most aggressive doubles team by moving them away from the net and can give the receiving pair an opportunity to counter attack. Even a lob return of service over the server's partner can set up an attacking move to the net. Never underestimate the value of the lob. It can be seen being put to good use in even the most high powered of men's doubles matches.

RETURN THE SERVICE
Make every effort to get the return of service back into play. Nothing can undermine a server's confidence more than having even his hardest serve returned into court. The return of service is a vital aspect of doubles play. Spend time perfecting a wide angled return, a low 'dink' shot or just simply a block return of service to the feet of the incoming server.

WIN YOUR SERVICE GAME
In theory the serving team should be at a great advantage as not only do they have the bonus of starting the rally off but the server's partner is in the most attacking

PRACTICAL PREPARATION

No matter how good your stroke technique, if your practical match preparation is poor then your performance will suffer.

EQUIPMENT
Before a match check that all your rackets are in a good state of repair and that the strings of your racket are not fraying. Always have a spare racket.

Check also that you have all your playing kit and pay particular attention to your shoes. Just as court surfaces vary so do the type of soles that you should wear to play on particular courts. Remember courts which have a loose top dressing will already be slippery and require shoes which give you extra grip whereas an indoor court surface requires a shoe which is fairly smooth so that the shoe will allow you to slide when necessary (see page 17).

Pay particular attention to your feet. Blisters on the feet are a mundane but common problem among tennis players and no matter how well you try if your feet are sore then you will not perform at your best. Always try to wear absorbent socks, preferably two pairs, and check your feet regularly for hard, caloused skin which should be removed at regular intervals.

WARM UP
Before playing a match or even undertaking a hard training session it is important that you do some form of warm up routine before you step on the court. This should consist of the following components:

1   A rigorous warm up of jogging and skipping to get you physically warm and make you start to perspire.

2   A routine of stretching exercises and mobility exercises to warm up your muscles to prevent injury.

3   Finally a sequence of moves similar to the ones you are about to use on the court. Now your body is ready to perform efficiently from the moment you play your first shot in earnest.

FITNESS TRAINING

This should form an important part of your long term strategy for improvement in matchplay. The ability to keep going is vital if you are to be a successful player; and while it is important to perfect stroke technique, it is also vitally important that you are sufficiently physically fit to withstand the demands of even the longest match.

The vital components of a recommended fitness training programme for tennis are listed below.

How to test your fitness level
Before starting a training programme try to find out your level of fitness by doing this simple test.

Run for twelve minutes and record the distance you have covered. After four weeks of training repeat and see if your distance has improved. It should have!

135

What type of training should you do?

Running Try building up to running for 15/20 minutes but start *gradually*. 5/10 minutes may be sufficient to begin with. *Fitness is not something that happens overnight.* You should try to run at a speed at which carrying on a conversation would just be possible – but only *just.*

Interval running Jog for 100 yards and then sprint for 50 yards. Repeat this at least ten times. You will find it quite demanding.

Court circuits If you have access to a tennis court try to do some sprinting and running on the court.

Set up a short running circuit which involves sprinting from one central position to six given spots on the court, and back. Record the time it takes you to do the circuit, rest for one minute and then repeat. Start with 2/3 court circuits and build up to 8/10 as your fitness improves.

Skipping Fast skipping is an excellent method of improving fitness but only if you can skip! Skip as fast as you can for thirty seconds, rest for thirty seconds and then repeat. Start with 2/3 circuits but increase to 8/10 as you improve.

How long should you train?

If you are an average player a training session lasting for approximately thirty minutes three times a week should be sufficient to show an increase in your fitness level. If you are a top level player a daily methodical programme for off-court training is essential.

Remember the aim is to improve your body's efficiency to pump oxygen-enriched blood round to the working muscles as quickly as possible. Therefore to gain benefit from your training you must exert yourself sufficiently hard to bring your pulse rate to some 70% of its maximum.

Strength training

It is important to build up well balanced body strength in *arms, trunk* and *legs* as these are all going to be worked hard in a demanding match.

Weight training A supervised weight training programme could certainly help you if you feel you lack body strength. However remember you don't want to produce just muscle bulk so weight training should be done under expert tuition and should be specific to your needs for tennis.

Exercise circuit A well planned exercise circuit for *arms, trunk* and *legs* should certainly be included in your fitness programme. Suggested exercises could be as follows:

ARM	ARM CIRCLING
TRUNK	SIT UPS
LEG	BURPEES
ARM	PRESS UPS
BODY	SWALLOWS
LEG	LONG JUMPS

Work at each exercise for one minute and count the number you achieve. Rest for two minutes between each exercise. Complete the six exercises and then find your *work rate* by halving the number you achieved. Having got your *work rate* for each exercise go through the circuit of six exercises and record the time. Rest for one minute and then repeat twice more.

Start with 2/3 circuits and build up to 4/5 as you improve.

Do this *twice a week*.

Speed Even though an individual's speed is essentially inanimate you should find that as your overall fitness improves so should your ability to move quickly.

Speed training requires quick bursts of speed for ten seconds with at least a fifty-second rest before the next burst of speed.

Court sprints are an excellent way of improving speed.

Do these at least 2/3 times a week. Sprint across the width of the court.

Suppleness
Finally, whether you are about to play a game of tennis or undertake a training session you must do 10/15 minutes of stretching and mobility exercises to maintain your suppleness.

This is essential to prevent injury and at least stiffness in muscles and joints.

Stretching exercises should be done for all the main muscle groups, namely: stretch each muscle for a count of 10/15 seconds. Gradually release the stretch and then repeat 3/4 times.

a Calves
b Quadriceps (front thigh)
c Hamstrings (back thigh)
d Adductors (inner thigh)
Joint mobilizing should include
a Head rotation
b Arm circling
c Trunk circling
d Ankle circling
Always start your stretching routine with some form of pulse warmer such as skipping or jogging. Finish with a more vigorous movement to prepare you for the activity ahead.

You need to build up stamina over a period of time. Therefore the hard endurance part of your training should be undertaken in the off season. Strength training is needed to build up the muscle strength required for tennis. Speed and suppleness are essential requirements for all successful players.

WARM DOWN

While it is important to undertake a fitness training programme and always do a warm up routine it is also essential to warm down after a strenuous match or training session. If you learn to take care of yourself then you should be able to enjoy many years of competitive play. Don't allow injury to force you out of the game!

Your warm down routine should be similar to your warm up routine. It allows the body to get rid of the lactic acid waste so often produced after strenuous exercise. Try to 'run down' with some stretching exercises and some gentle jogging. Finally enjoy your post match shower. You should have deserved it!

MENTAL PREPARATION

Perhaps the most important aspect of any match is the mental side. No matter how good your on court preparation and your warm up routine all can be lost if you are not in a good mental state to play your match. Concentration can be the most elusive quality of all and can so easily be lost in times of stress. All players will 'lose their cool' on occasions. The important thing is to try to recognise what can upset you. It is easy for onlookers to criticize players who lose their tempers, but it is not so easy to understand the tensions and stresses that can build up during a match which you desperately want to win.

Perhaps the most important thing for any player to remember is that the most difficult opponent to beat is YOU. Try to exclude self destructive thoughts from your mind. Concentrate on playing the ball and beating the opponent at the other side of the net. Look to see how he is taking the pressure rather than worrying about what is 'blowing up' inside your own head.

Advisers will tell you that if you have prepared well, worked out a sound match plan and done your warm up routine you will be well prepared for the match ahead. This may well be true but it still doesn't cope with the problems that can arise during the match. The dramas that can go on in your mind can so easily affect the outcome. The more you can stop any conscious thought other than what you are doing with the ball the better will be your 'match cool'!

Forget the poor call which has 'robbed' you of that crucial game. Try to play each point as it comes, concentrate on the ball

Boris Becker's famous gesture of triumph reveals the intensity of his determination to win.

and what you plan to do with it. Players often talk of a 'cocoon of concentration' which excludes them from any thoughts other than the game in hand. If you are able to reach this 'ideal state' then you are well on the way to being a match winner.

However, if you find you are unable to concentrate and are giving way to the outside irritations try to think of the following points:

1 Concentrate on WATCHING THE BALL.
2 Keep to a SIMPLE match plan.
3 Keep the ball in play.

4 Keep to the simple tactics already mentioned.
5 Keep thinking POSITIVELY.

STRESS

If you enjoy competing and enjoy the challenge of the cut and thrust of matchplay then you should have no problems with stress.

Sometimes outside influences can upset a player, making him reach for goals that are too high too soon. The inevitable failure can cause a sudden loss of confidence.

Try to judge your progress in tennis by setting yourself short and long term goals. Regard these as 'stepping stones' towards your ultimate goal. Remember not everyone has the ability or even the inclination to be a Wimbledon Champion, but if you realize *your own potential* whatever that may be then you should be satisfied with your success and you will have become a *winner*.

SHORT TERM GOALS

When you are working at your stroke technique it is worth setting yourself minor goals to see how you are progressing. For instance you may still be a novice competitor, but if one of your short term goals is to get every first service into court, and you manage to do this then, even if you lose the match, you have achieved your shorter goal. It is important to realize that novice competitors may well lose far more matches than they are likely to win but by setting yourself realistic goals within the

McEnroe loses his cool

match context you can build constructively and positively on your game for the future.

LONG TERM GOALS

While your short term goal can be likened to a stepping stone, your long term goals should be regarded as rest platforms on your ladder to success. Again set yourself a number of medium and long term goals and enjoy attaining them. Confidence in your own ability to succeed is one of the most important aspects of the successful competitor. Don't be too hard on yourself and set too difficult a target which you may never reach. Set *realistic* goals to build your self confidence.

Achievement is an important aspect of a player's development. Savour your triumphs and in moments of stress relive the better moments. Mentally rehearse the strokes you are about to play and the tactics you are about to use. Imagine yourself in the match itself and try to get rid of any inhibitions you may have about performing in front of a crowd even before you get out on the court!

Try not to overestimate the strength of your opponent. He may be feeling as insecure as you. If you can face the *dragon* in your mind before you encounter the live situation on court you will find you are better prepared and the *dragon* may not be there at all. Approach matches in a positive frame of mind with a clear simple match plan.

LEARNING HOW TO LEARN

A good tennis player never stops learning, and the modern game never stops changing. Rackets and court surfaces are altered frequently as technology develops. Players must learn how to adapt to these ever changing conditions. If you are to adapt you must study the game widely, as well as playing it! Try to visit any major tournament which is held in your area. Watch as much tennis as you can on television. Notice the varying styles of play among the top players and study their individual interpretation of use of spin and tactical awareness. Try to become a good mimic, and having watched the top players in action go out and imagine that you are

playing in the same way. Remember children learn by copying. Tennis players can learn by copying too!

Obviously good coaching should help you to make a more rapid improvement in your game but *do* sift the advice that you are given and make certain that you really understand what you are being asked to do.

Learn from your matches and assess where you need to improve. Try to get someone to watch your matchplay, as sometimes what is glaringly obvious to the spectator may go totally unnoticed by the player himself. Be prepared to take advice and listen to constructive criticism.

Watch the top players. Lendl plays an attacking forehand

LEARNING HOW TO PRACTISE

Try to get a sensible balance between matchplay, practice and physical training. All are vital components of the complete tennis player.

In order to build up confidence in your stroke technique, you must play regularly. Obviously if you become a full time tennis player then tennis will be your life. Many of us however have to fit tennis in to an already overcrowded day and so it is important to establish how much time you can reasonably put into your game. Is tennis part of your life or life itself?

Once you have planned how many hours you can spend on your tennis it is important to divide your time between practice

141

and matchplay. It is not always easy to get either the ideal practice partner or even a practice wall where you can do some solo drills.

Perhaps you have a willing parent or friend who would be happy to help with your tennis but who is not a tennis player himself. Practice with a non player may not be perfect but it can be of great benefit if you have a large supply of tennis balls and a willing hand thrower aiming to a given target area.

TYPES OF PRACTICE

SOLO
Against a wall or practice netting. Against a ball machine on a tennis court. In both cases, aim for target areas.

WITH A PARTNER (non player)
Using a ball hopper and a good supply of tennis balls get your non playing practice partner to feed the ball to given target areas on the court. Set yourself a target for your shots and move back to a set area after you have played each shot. If the non player now shortens the intervals between throws you can artificially simulate a rally.

WITH A PARTNER (player)
Use some of the practice drills outlined in early sections.

Start simply and build up the exercise as your control improves.

Remember you need to hit tennis balls in great QUANTITY if you are to improve your ball control; but all practice must have QUALITY.

Having done the set routines progress to competition within the routine.

Start to link shots together, i.e. drive from the back of the court, move in on an approach drive and try to win from the net.

Finally play some form of loaded 'conditioned' game which may restrict a player to hitting into a certain area of the court in order to practise a particular aspect of the game, i.e. service and return and then rally only in the forehand areas of the court hitting diagonal shots.

WITH OPPONENTS
Always allocate some of your practice time to playing matches. Try to have a variety of opponents as you can learn so much by competing against differing styles of play. Never underestimate the value of playing against an unorthodox player. While it is good to be on court with a sound tennis player who has good ball control, the unorthodox player can test your tactical thinking and your ability to control your shots in a less predictable situation.

SINGLES AND DOUBLES PLAY
Strike a balance between playing singles and doubles matches. It may not always be easy to get a court just to play singles; but try not to play doubles all the time. But do play some doubles matches, as this can develop your stroke variations and tactical thinking.

COMPETITIVE PLAY

View competitive play as an essential stepping stone towards your long term goals. Schools, clubs, counties, regions, all provide competitive events for all ages, ranging from the young children who compete at short tennis to the veteran and vintage age groups.

ENJOYMENT!

Finally remember that whether playing or practising, your tennis should be *fun*! Hopefully this book will have stimulated your ideas so that you may gain further enjoyment from the game.

Mandlikova enjoying her tennis

ADDRESSES

The Lawn Tennis Association,
Barons Court,
West Kensington,
London W14 9EG
Tel: 01 385 2366

The Scottish Lawn Tennis Association,
12 Melville Crescent,
Edinburgh EH3 7LU
Tel: 031 225 1284

The Welsh Lawn Tennis Association,
The National Sports Centre for Wales,
Sophia Gardens,
Cardiff
Tel: 0222 371 838

Professional Tennis Coaches Association
of Great Britain,
21, Glenlairn Court,
Lansdowne Road,
Cheltenham,
Glos. GL50 2NB
Tel: 0242 524701

Information regarding tennis in Australia
may be obtained from:

LTA of Australia,
Box 343,
South Yarra
Victoria 3141,
Australia

in Canada:

Canadian Tennis Association,
3111 Steeles Avenue West,
Downsview,
Ontario,
Canada M3J 3H2

other countries:

The International Tennis Federation,
Church Road,
Wimbledon,
London,
SW19 5TF

First published in Great Britain 1986 by
Pan Books Ltd,
Cavaye Place, London SW10 9PG

9 8 7 6 5 4 3 2 1

© Lawn Tennis Association 1986
Photographs © Tommy Hindley 1986
Designed by Peter Ward

ISBN 0 330 29171 8 paperback
ISBN 0 330 29660 4 hardback

Photoset by Parker Typesetting Service, Leicester
Printed and bound in Great Britain by
R. J. Acford, Chichester, Sussex